A Programmer's Guide to Computer Science

William M. Springer II, PhD

A Programmer's Guide to Computer Science

By William M. Springer II

Published by Jaxson Media, Madison, WI, United States of America

Visit the author's website at `http://www.whatwill iamsaid.com/books/`.

ISBN: 978-1-951204-03-7

Library of Congress Control Number: 2019909527

First Edition, First Printing, 2019

Cover design and robot graphics by Brit Springer at Moonlight Designs Studio - `https://moonlightdesigns studio.com/`. Typesetting and other graphics done by the author in LaTeX. Technical editing by Nicholas R Allgood. Copy editing by Margo Simon.

Special thanks to Øyvind Jakobsson, Josh Earl, Jed Reynolds, Fiona Holder, Sable Schwab, and others who provided feedback during the process. Along with the people mentioned above, they've made this a better book.

Contents

III   Non-Graph Algorithms   103

IV   Problem-Solving Techniques   119

V   Complexity Theory   137

Introduction

Why this book?

The developers I know come from a wide variety of backgrounds. Some have graduate degrees in computer science; others studied photography, math, or don't even have a college degree.

Over the last few years I've noticed more of a desire from working programmers to learn computer science for a number of reasons:

- To improve as programmers

- To get past the algorithms questions that often serve as gatekeepers for programming jobs

- To satisfy an interest in computer science or alleviate regret at never having had the opportunity to study the subject

This book is for all of you.

While many people will find the topics covered here interesting in their own right, I've attempted to also show where this knowledge is useful in real-world (non-academic) situations. The goal is that when you've finished this book, you will know the basics of what you would have learned from an undergraduate computer science degree and how to apply it.

Simply put, this book aims to make you a better, more knowledgeable programmer through a greater understanding of computer science. I can't consolidate two decades of college and professional experience into one book... but I can try to hit the good parts. My hope is that you will find at least one concept where you can say "yeah, that makes sense now" and apply it to your everyday work.

What the book is not

The point of this book is to make the reader more comfortable with computer science concepts and how to apply them, rather than to fully replicate four years of study.

In particular, this is not a book on proofs. While part VIII in Volume II covers proof techniques, standard algorithms are generally given without proofs of correctness. The idea is that the reader will emerge knowing of the existence of these algorithms and how to use them, without getting bogged down in the fine details. For a book of proofs, written at the graduate level, I highly recommend *Introduction to Algorithms* by Cormen, Leiserson, Rivest, and Stein, generally referred to as CLRS. More in-depth reading material is often referenced in the footnotes as well.

This is also not a book on programming; you won't find a discussion of when to use integers vs doubles or an explanation of loops. Indeed, it is expected that the reader will be able to understand pseudocode listings used to describe algorithms[1]. The intent is to tie computer science concepts to programming practices that are already familiar to the reader.

Additional resources

I've included references to additional material in the footnotes for the reader who wishes to dive deeper into a particular subject. Additionally, self-assessment quizzes for each chapter are available for download at `http://www.whatwilliamsaid.com/books/`.

---

[1]All of the code in this book is C-based pseudocode.

Part I

Computer Science
Fundamentals

Chapter 1

Asymptotic Runtime

1.1 What is an algorithm?

Suppose you were teaching a robot to make a peanut butter sandwich. Your instructions might go something like this:

1. Open the top left cabinet.

2. Pick up the peanut butter jar and remove it from the cabinet.

3. Close the cabinet.

4. Hold the peanut butter jar in your left hand and grasp the lid in your right hand.

5. Turn your right hand counter-clockwise until the lid comes off the jar.

6. And so on...

Figure 1.1: A sandwich-making robot

This is a program: you define every step that the computer needs to take and specify all the information the computer requires to execute each step. On the other hand, suppose you're telling a person how to make a peanut butter sandwich. Your instructions might be more like this:

- Get out the peanut butter, jelly, and bread.

- Use a knife to spread peanut butter on one slice of bread.

- Use a spoon to spread jelly on a second slice of bread.

- Put the two slices together. Enjoy!

This is an algorithm: a process to follow to reach the desired outcome (in this case, a peanut butter and jelly sandwich). Notice that the algorithm is much more abstract than the program. The program tells the robot exactly where to find the items needed in this particular kitchen, with every relevant detail specified. It is an implementation of the algorithm, which provides all the important details, but can be run on any hardware (a kitchen, in this case) that has the required elements (peanut butter, jelly, bread, and silverware).

1.2   Why speed matters

Modern computers are fast enough that in many cases, the speed of an algorithm isn't particularly important. If I press a button and it takes the computer 1/25 of a second to react rather than 1/100 of a second, the difference doesn't matter to me - from my point of view the computer is responding instantly in either case.

But there are many applications where speed continues to be important, particularly when dealing with a large number of items that need to be manipulated. For example, suppose you have a list of a million items which need to be sorted. If an efficient sort takes one second, an inefficient sort could take several weeks. One can see how the user might not want to wait for this to complete.

We often describe a problem as being intractable if there is no known way to solve it in a reasonable amount of time, where "reasonable" depends on various real-life factors. For example, the security of data encryption often depends on the difficulty of factoring large numbers. If I send you an encrypted message, and I need to keep the contents secret for a week, then it doesn't matter to me if an adversary intercepts the message and knows of a way to decrypt it given three years of effort. The problem is not insolvable - the eavesdropper simply doesn't know how to solve it quickly enough for the solution to be useful.

One important skill in computer programming is optimizing only those parts of the program that need to be optimized. If part of the user interface is one thousandth of a second slower than it could be, nobody cares - in this case, we would choose a more readable program over an unnoticeable increase in speed. On the other hand, the code inside of a loop that may be executed millions of times should be written as efficiently as possible.

1.3   When seconds (don't) count

Consider our sandwich-making algorithm from section 1.1. Because we want the algorithm to be usable by any number of different sandwich-making robots, we don't want to measure the time the algorithm takes in seconds, as this will vary from robot to robot. One robot may take longer than another to open a cabinet, but be better at opening a jar of peanut butter.

Rather then trying to measure the actual speed of each step, which would differ between robots and kitchens, we find it more useful to count (and minimize) the number of steps. For example, an algorithm that requires that the robot gets the knife and spoon at the same time would likely be more efficient than one in which it opens the silverware drawer, gets the knife, closes the drawer, puts the knife on the counter, opens the drawer again, gets the spoon...

Measuring Time: Algorithm vs Program

Remember that algorithms are more general than programs. For our sandwich-making algorithm, we want to count steps. If we were to actually employ a specific sandwich-making robot, then we would be more interested in the exact amount of time it requires to make each sandwich.

We also need to recognize that not all steps will require the same amount of time; getting out the knife is likely to be faster than spreading peanut butter over the bread. Because of this, we're less interested in knowing the exact number of steps required than we are in having a general idea of how many steps will be required relative to the size of the input. In the case of our robot, the amount of time required to make a sandwich does not increase as we make more sandwiches (provided we don't run out of jelly).

In actual computer terms, two given computers may vary in how quickly they can run an algorithm depending on clock speed, amount of available memory, clock cycles required for a given instruction, etc. They will, however, tend to require approximately the same number of instructions, and we can measure the rate at which the number of instructions required increases with the problem size. For example, given an array of numbers to be sorted, providing an array a thousand times as large might require a thousand times as many instructions for one algorithm and a million times as many for another[1].

---

[1]See chapter 8 for specific examples.

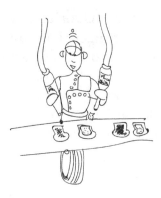

Figure 1.2: A more efficient sandwich-making robot

Often we wish to measure the speed of an algorithm in several different ways. In a life-or-death situation - for example, firing thrusters in a probe attempting to land on Mars - we want to know the worst-case runtime. We may wish to choose an algorithm which is slightly slower on average for a guarantee that it will never take longer than we find acceptable (and crash our probe instead of landing it). For more everyday scenarios, we may be willing to accept the occasional spike in runtime if it keeps the average time down; when playing a video game, for example, we might prefer to generate results more quickly on average at the cost of needing to abort the occasional long-running calculation. And there may be times when we would like to know the absolute best case performance. In most cases, however, we'll just calculate the worst-case runtime, which is often equal to the average-case runtime anyway.

1.4 How we describe speed

Suppose we have two different lists of integers that we would like to sort. List one is {1,2,3,4,5,6,7,8} and list two is {3,5,4,1,2}. Which list will take less time to sort?

The answer is that we don't know. For one sorting algorithm, the fact that the first list is already sorted will allow it to return almost immediately. For another, the fact that the second list is shorter may be the determining factor. But notice that two properties of the input - the size of the list and the order in which the integers appear - affect the number of steps required for the lists to be sorted.

If a particular property, such as being already sorted, affects the runtime of a particular algorithm by only a constant amount, we can often ignore it because the impact is not noticeable when compared to the impact of the problem size. For example, suppose that our robot can make a sandwich with either grape or raspberry jelly, and the raspberry jar takes slightly longer to open. If the robot is making a million sandwiches, the slight impact of the jelly selection on the total sandwich-making time is dwarfed by the number of sandwiches required, so we can ignore it and simply say that making a million sandwiches takes approximately a million times as long as making one sandwich.

In mathematical terms, we are finding the *asymptotic* runtime of the algorithm, which is the rate at which the runtime grows compared to the size of the input. For our sandwich-making robot, it takes some constant c amount of time to make one sandwich and n times as long, or cn time, to make n sandwiches. We drop the constant and simply say that our sandwich algorithm is $O(n)$ (pronounced "big oh of n", or just "oh of n"), which means that the worst-case runtime is proportional to the number of sandwiches to be made. We aren't interested in the exact number of steps required, but in the rate at which this number increases as the problem size (in this case, the number of sandwiches) grows.

1.5   Common algorithm speeds

As our robot makes more sandwiches, this does not increase the amount of time required for any one sandwich. This is a *linear* algorithm, in which the total runtime is proportional to the number of items to be processed. For most problems, this is the absolute best you can do[2]. A common example in programming would be reading in a list of items and performing some task on each one, where the time taken to process an item doesn't depend on any other item. We have a loop that does a constant amount of work and executes once for each of the n items, so it takes $O(n)$ time.

More often, the number of items on the list affects the amount of work that needs to be performed for each item. A sorting algorithm may process every node of the list while dividing it into two smaller lists and repeat until every element is in its own list. At each iteration it does $O(n)$ work and it requires $O(\lg n)$ iterations, for a total of $O(n) \times O(\lg n) = O(n \lg n)$ time.

---

[2]Because n is the size of the input, it generally takes $O(n)$ time just to read in the input.

Math Alert

A logarithm describes to what power a base number must be raised in order to get the desired value. For example, $\log_{10} 1000 = 3$, because $10^3 = 1000$.

In computers we're often dividing by two, so we commonly use base-two logarithms. The shorthand for $\log_2 n$ is $\lg n$. So $\lg 1 = 0$, $\lg 2 = 1$, $\lg 4 = 2$, $\lg 8 = 3$, etc.

Runtimes get worse from there. Consider an algorithm where every element in a collection must be compared to every other element in the collection - we do $O(n)$ work $O(n)$ times, for a total of $O(n^2)$, or *quadratic* time.

All of these algorithms, where the runtime is proportional to the size of the input raised to some power, are known as *polynomial* algorithms; these are generally considered to be "fast" algorithms. Of course, an algorithm where the solution is proportional to the 100th power of the size of the input, while polynomial, would not be considered fast by any stretch of the imagination! In practice, however, problems which are known to have polynomial time solutions can generally be solved in *quartic* (4th power) time or better.

This doesn't mean that an asymptotically more efficient algorithm will always run more quickly than an asymptotically less efficient algorithm. For example, suppose your hard drive crashes and you've lost some important files. Fortunately, you had them backed up online[3].

---

[3]I used numbers from Carbonite cloud backup for this example,

You can download your files from the cloud at the rate of 10Mbps (assuming you have a good connection). This is linear time – the amount of time it takes to retrieve all of your lost files is (more or less) directly proportional to the size of those files. The backup service also offers an option to have your files loaded onto an external drive and shipped to you – this is a constant-time solution, or $O(1)$, because it will take the same amount of time to receive your data no matter how big it is[4]. If you only have a few megabytes of files to restore, downloading them is clearly much faster, but once you reach the size that will require as long to download as to ship, the external drive will always be faster as the size of your data keeps growing.

If polynomial algorithms are fast, what algorithms are slow? For some algorithms (known as *exponential* algorithms), the number of operations is bounded by some constant raised to the size of the input, rather than by the size of the input raised to some constant. For example, consider trying to guess a numeric passcode of length n. Assuming there are 10 digits (0-9), the number of possible codes is 10^n. Notice that this grows **much** more quickly than n^{10} - when n is only 20, the polynomial algorithm is already almost 10 million times faster!

---

although there are many others. This is in no way an endorsement – they were just the first service that popped up when I searched.

[4]Well, relatively constant – it takes 1-3 business days. Constant in this sense doesn't mean that something always takes the same amount of time, only that the runtime does not depend on the size of the input. We also assume that the backup company can get your copy ready quickly enough that having a very large file doesn't cause them to miss the next mail drop.

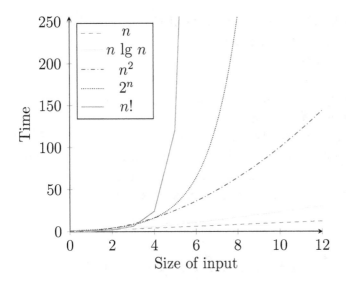

Figure 1.3: Even on small inputs, differences in asymptotic runtime quickly become noticeable.

1.6 Is polynomial always better?

As a general rule, computer scientists are interested in polynomial solutions to problems, particularly solutions that run in quadratic time or better. However, given a reasonable (small) problem size, exponential algorithms can be worthwhile.

In many cases, we can determine an approximate solution to a problem in polynomial time, but only know how to find an exact (or close to exact) answer in exponential time. For example, consider the traveling salesman problem, where the salesman would like to visit every city on his route exactly once and return home, while traveling the shortest possible distance. (Imagine how much money UPS or FedEx can save if they make their routes just slightly more efficient!)

We can get an exact answer by calculating every possible route and comparing the total distances, but there are $O(n!)$ possible paths. A very close solution (within less than 1% of optimal) can be found in exponential time[5], but a possibly 'good enough' (within 50% of optimal) solution can be found in polynomial time[6]. This is the usual trade-off: we may be able to get a reasonably good approximation quickly or a more exact answer slowly.

1.7 Runtime of an algorithm

Consider the following code:

```
foreach (name in NameCollection)
{
        Print "Hello, {name}!";
}
```

Here we have a collection of n strings; for each string, we print a short message. Printing the message takes a constant amount of time[7], or $O(1)$, and we do it n times, or $O(n)$. Multiplying these together, we can see that this code runs in $O(n)$ time.

---

[5]For a comprehensive look at various approaches, see *The Traveling Salesman Problem* by Applegate, Bixby, Chvátal, and Cook.

[6]As of this writing, there are known algorithms to find a solution no worse than 50% larger than optimal in $O(n^3)$ time. See, e.g., "Shorter Tours by Nicer Ears" by Sebo and Vygen, 2012.

[7]Again, not meaning that it takes exactly the same amount of time for each string, only that the time required for each one is not affected by the number of strings.

How about this function?

```
DoStuff(numbers)
{
   sum=0;
   foreach (num in numbers)
   {
      sum += num;
   }
   product=1;
   foreach (num in numbers)
   {
      product *= num;
   }
   Print "The sum is {sum} and the
      product is {product}";
}
```

In this case, we have two loops; each one consists of an $O(n)$ loop that does a constant amount of work, or $O(n)$ total for each. Adding up $O(n)$ and $O(n)$, we drop the constant and again get $O(n)$ – not $O(2n)$. Consider that the above function could also have been written like so:

```
DoStuff(numbers)
{
   sum=0, product=1;
   foreach (num in numbers)
   {
      sum += num;
      product *= num;
   }
    Print "The sum is {sum} and the
       product is {product}";
```

```
}
```

Now we have only one loop, which again does a constant amount of work; it's simply a larger constant than before. The thing to remember is that we're interested in how quickly the runtime grows as the problem size increases, rather than the exact number of operations for a given problem size.

Let's try something a little more complex. What is the runtime of this algorithm?

```
CountInventory(stuffToSell, colorList)
{
   totalItems = 0;
   foreach (thing in stuffToSell)
   {
      foreach (color in colorList)
      {
         totalItems += thing[color];
      }
   }
}
```

In this case, we have two loops, but one is nested inside the other so we will multiply the runtimes rather than adding them. The outer loop runs once for each item in our catalog, and the inner loop runs once for each color we provide. If we have n items and m colors, then the total runtime is $O(nm)$. Notice that it is NOT $O(n^2)$; we have no reason to think that n and m are in any way related.

Here's another function:

```
doesStartWith47(numbers)
{
```

```
   return (numbers[0]==47);
}
```

This function checks to see whether or not the first element of an array of integers is equal to 47, and returns the result. The amount of work it does is not dependent on the size of the input, and so it is $O(1)$[8].

We often write programs that involve binary searches, which means that our analysis will involve logarithms. For example, consider the following[9]:

```
binarySearch(numarray, left, right, x)
{
   if (left > right) { return -1; }
   int mid = 1 + (right - 1)/2;
   if (numarray[mid]==x) { return mid; }
   if (numarray[mid]>x)
       { return binarySearch(numarray,
           left, mid-1, x); }
   return binarySearch(numarray, mid+1,
      right, x);
}
```

Given a sorted array, we look to see if the middle element of the array is what we're searching for. If so, we return the index of the midpoint. If not, and the midpoint is larger than the desired value, we recurse on the first half of the array. Otherwise, we recurse on the second half. For each recursive call we do a constant amount of work (checking that left isn't greater than right, which

---

[8]This is, of course, assuming that the array is passed in by reference; if it's passed by value this would be $O(n)$.

[9]Good programming practice would be to move the left>right check to the end because it's the less common case, but we'll do it like this here to avoid nesting.

would imply we've searched the entire array and our desired value is not to be found, then calculating the midpoint and comparing that value at that location to what we're looking for). We make O(lg n) calls, each of which takes O(1) time, so binary search is O(lg n).

Advanced Topics

Suppose you have a recursive function which breaks your problem into two parts, each of which is 2/3 the size of the original? We actually have a formula for calculating recursions like this; see chapter 31 on the Master Theorem.

1.8   How hard is a problem?

When we have an algorithm to solve a problem, it's often fairly straightforward to determine the runtime of that algorithm. What happens when we don't have an algorithm yet, but still need to get an idea of how difficult it will be to solve the problem?

We can do this by comparing problems to other, similar problems with known runtimes. We divide problems into classes, which are sets of problems that have similar characteristics. The two main classes that we're interested in are problems that can be solved in polynomial time and problems whose solutions can be checked in polynomial time. We'll discuss both of these in the next chapter.

Chapter 2

Data Structures

2.1 Organizing data

Data structures are one of the foundational parts of computer science[1]. When we discuss the runtime of various algorithms[2], we assume the data is stored in an appropriate structure that allows it to be handled efficiently. Which structure is best depends on the type of data and how it will be accessed.

- Do we need random access, or is sequential access sufficient?

- Will we always append data when writing, or do we need to be able to insert values as well?

---

[1] Much of this is likely to be review to the experienced programmer, but because it is so important to what follows we include it anyway. Feel free to skim this chapter if you are already familiar with the material.

[2] See chapters 1, 31, and 32.

- Are duplicate values allowed?

- Do we prefer the lowest possible access time or a strict upper bound on how long a given operation can take?

The answers to each of these questions play a role in how the data should be stored.

2.2 Arrays, queues, and other ways to line up

Perhaps the most familiar data structure, an array is a collection of elements indexed by a key. The elements are stored sequentially, with the key taking the form of an offset from the starting location in memory, so that we can calculate the location of any element given its key. This is why array indices[3] generally start with zero; the first element of an array is zero elements away from the start, the next is one element away from the start, and so on. "One element away" could be a byte, word, etc., depending on the size of the data; the important thing is that a consistent amount of space is allocated for each element of the array.

Arrays are useful because retrieving or storing any element takes constant time, and the entire array takes $O(n)$ space[4]. When the number of elements is known in advance, there is no wasted space; all locations are simply

---

[3]Both "indexes" and "indices" are accepted plurals of the word "index"; we use "array indices" and "database indexes".

[4]Recall that unless stated otherwise, n is the number of elements.

offsets from the start, so we don't use any of the allocated space for pointers. Because all elements in the array occupy contiguous memory locations, iterating through the array is likely to be noticeably faster than iterating over many other data structures due to fewer cache misses[5].

On the other hand, that requirement for a contiguous block of memory can make arrays a poor choice when the number of elements is not known, as increasing the array size may mean copying the entire array to a different memory location (assuming one exists) and avoiding this issue by pre-allocating much more space than needed can be quite wasteful[6]. The other major issue is that inserting and deleting elements is very time consuming ($O(n)$), as every element may need to be moved.

In practice, arrays are used both on their own and to implement many other data structures that place additional restrictions on how the data is manipulated. A string, for example, may be implemented as an array of characters. A queue is a sequential list where elements are only added to one end (enqueue) and removed from the other (dequeue); it can thus be implemented using an array where the "start" moves around with the front of the queue, provided that the maximum number of items in the queue never exceeds the size of the array. However, a queue of indeterminate length may be better implemented using a doubly-linked list (section 2.3). Other

---

[5]This is "locality of reference": the idea that once we've accessed an item, it's likely that other items stored nearby will be accessed as well in the near future. Since we've already loaded the page containing the first item into the cache, retrieving the nearby items (which are probably found on the same page) is faster.

[6]This is particularly an issue when dealing with embedded systems, which tend to have a limited amount of memory.

structures implemented using arrays include lists, stacks and heaps (section 2.4), priority queues (which are often implemented with heaps), and hash tables (section 2.5)

2.3   Linked lists

A linked list is a data structure where every element contains both data and a pointer to the next element in the list (and, if it is a doubly-linked list, to the previous element). A pointer to a linked list is simply a pointer to the first element, or head, of the list; as the elements may be scattered anywhere in the allocated memory, finding a specified element requires starting at the head and walking through the list.

We've mentioned that many data structures are implemented using either an array or a linked list. In many ways a linked list is the complement of an array. Where the strength of an array is fast access to any item (given its key), finding an element of the list requires walking through the links until the desired element is found, in worst case $O(n)$ time. On the other hand, while an array is fixed in size, because the elements of a linked list can be anywhere in memory, it can grow arbitrarily until the available memory is exhausted. Additionally, while insertions and deletions are very expensive in an array, they can be done in constant time in a linked list if we have a pointer to the previous node.

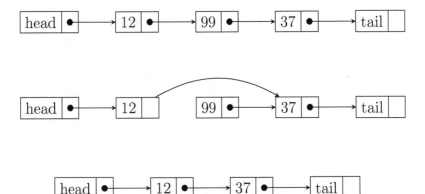

Figure 2.1: Deleting a node from a linked list

Real-World Application

Consider a train as an example of a doubly-linked list. Each car in the train is connected to the previous car and (if it exists) to the next one. Cars can be easily added to the end of the train, but you can also add cars to the middle of the train by unlinking and relinking the existing cars around the ones to be added, or you can unlink cars in the middle, send them off down a side track, and relink the remaining cars. However, a car cannot be retrieved directly; you must first traverse the train and separate it from the car in front of it.

Theoretical Silliness

I had a professor once who asked the class how to determine whether a linked list contains a cycle. There are several classic solutions to this problem. One is to reverse the node pointers as we traverse them; if a loop exists, you will eventually return to the head of the list. Another is to traverse the list with two pointers, with one pointer moving by one node at a time and the other by two nodes; if there exists a cycle, then the two pointers will eventually point to the same node.

However, the professor specifically said that he didn't care how bad the runtime of our method was, so I offered this bit of silliness: calculate the memory required to hold one node of the list and divide into the total memory of the system. Keep a running total of how many nodes have been visited. If the number of nodes visited exceeds the number of distinct nodes that could possibly be stored, the list must contain a cycle.

This solution has the dual advantages of taking a ridiculously long time (it's bounded by the size of the memory rather than the size of the list) and being absolutely correct.

2.4 Stacks and heaps

2.4.1 Stacks

A *stack* is a LIFO (last in, first out) data structure in which elements are only added to or removed from the top; we say that we push an item on the stack or pop it from the stack.

A stack can be implemented with an array (keeping track of the current length of the stack) or with a singly-linked list (keeping track of the head of the list[7]). As with queues, the array implementation is more straightforward but puts a limit on the size of the stack, while a linked list implementation can grow as long as memory is available.

Stacks support four basic operations, each of which can be implemented to run in $O(1)$ time: push (add an item), pop (remove an item), isEmpty (check whether the stack is empty), and size (get the number of items on the stack). Often we will also implement peek (look at the top item on the stack but do not remove it) which is equivalent to popping the top item and then pushing it again.

Pushing an item on the stack will throw an exception if the stack has limited size and is currently full (overflow error), while popping an item will throw an exception if the stack is currently empty (underflow error).

While stacks do not allow for random access, they work well for many operations in computing that require maintaining a history, from the Undo operation to recursive function calls. In this case, the stack provides backtracking, where we need to revert to a prior state. In section 13.3, we will see how stacks are used to implement pushdown automata, which recognize context-free languages. In section 23.3, we discuss how memory is allocated on the stack or the heap.

A common example of using a stack is checking for balanced braces. Consider a language in which braces

---

[7]Rather than adding new items to the end of the list, we can just append them to the beginning. When we pop an item, it will always be the first element in the list.

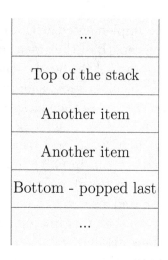

...
Top of the stack
Another item
Another item
Bottom - popped last
...

Figure 2.2: Items are always
pushed on or popped off the top
of the stack.

must come in pairs; that is, every right brace (}) is preceded by a matching left brace ({). We can read in a
string and, every time a left brace is encountered, we
push it on the stack. Every time a right brace is encountered, we pop a left brace off the stack. If we ever try to
pop a brace from the stack and find it empty, then there
is a right brace without a matching left brace preceding
it. If the stack is not empty at the end of the string, then
we read more left braces than right braces. Otherwise,
all braces in the string come in pairs.

2.4.2 Heaps

Heaps also tend to be implemented with arrays. Like the
stack, only one element of the heap can be removed at
a time, but rather than the most recently added element

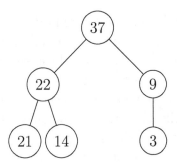

Figure 2.3: Sibling nodes in a heap (those with the same parent) have no particular relation; each node is simply lower priority than its parent.

it will be the maximum element (for a max-heap) or the minimum element (for a min-heap). The heap is partially ordered based on the key of each element, such that the highest (or lowest) priority element is always stored at the root.

The word *heap* refers to a data structure which satisfies the heap ordering property, either min-heap (the value of each node is no smaller than the value of its parent) or max-heap (the value of each node is no larger than the value of its parent). If it is not specified otherwise, when speaking of a heap we mean a binary heap, which is a complete binary tree[8] that satisfies the heap ordering property; other useful types include leftist heaps, binomial heaps, and fibonacci heaps.

A max-heap supports the operations find-max (peek), insert (push), extract-max (pop), and increase-key (change

---

[8]This is a binary tree in which every level, except possibly the bottom level, has the maximum number of nodes; trees are discussed in detail in chapter 4.

a node's key and then move the node to its new position in the graph). After the heap is created from a list of items, in $O(n)$ time, each of these operations requires $O(\log n)$ time on a binary heap[9].

Heaps are used when you need quick access to the largest (or smallest) item on a list without the overhead of keeping the rest of the list sorted. This is why they are used to implement priority queues: we only care about what's next in line (always the current root of the heap), not about the relative order of everything else. We cover heaps in more detail in sections 5.3 and 6.5.

2.5 Hash tables

Suppose you wish to determine whether an array contains a particular element. If the array is sorted, you can do a binary search to locate the element in $O(\log n)$ time; if not, you can scan the entire array in $O(n)$ time. Of course, if you knew where the item was, you could go there directly, in $O(1)$ time.

In some cases, such as counting sort (section 8.4.1), the element to be stored (or its key) is used as an index into the array, so we can just go to the desired location without searching. What if, for an arbitrary object, we had a function that takes that object's key and converts it to an array index, so we know exactly where the object should be stored? This is how hash tables work.

The first part of a hash table is the hash function; it converts the key of the element to be placed into a hash that then maps to a specified spot in the table.

---

[9]For details on the time complexity of each operation, see *Introduction to Algorithms* by Cormen et al.

For example, suppose that our keys are a set of strings and the hash function maps each string to the number of characters in that string[10]. Then "cat" would go in cell 3 and "penguin" would go in cell 7. If we have a limited amount of space, then we take the hash mod the size of the array; if the array is limited to ten spots (0-9), then the string "sesquipedalophobia" (which has a hash of 18) would go into spot 7[11,12].

What happens when we've already placed "cat" and then try to insert "cat" again? We only allow one copy of each item; for some implementations we keep a counter at each location and increment it as needed to track the number of copies of that item. On the other hand, suppose we try to insert "dog", which maps to the same location; there are two ways we can handle this. We may treat each location as being a bucket of objects, represented as a linked list (which we'll have to search through to find the correct pet); this is called chaining. Or we may walk the dog through nearby locations until we find an empty spot for it; this is called open addressing. With chaining, the size of the table is unlimited but performance will degrade as the number of elements in a given spot increases. With open addressing, the table has a fixed maximum size; once all spots are filled, no additional elements can be inserted.

How we set up the hash table depends on whether we

---

[10]It's not a very good hash function.

[11]If we hashed both "sesquipedalophobia" and "hippopotomonstrosesquippedaliophobia" mod 9, both would go into spot zero and collide, to the delight of any watching word enthusiasts and the abject horror of anyone with logophobia.

[12]In practice, we would use an array whose size is a prime number.

prefer to minimize collisions (multiple values that map to the same spot) or storage space. As the size of the allocated space increases relative to the number of values to be inserted, the odds of collision decrease. What we gain, at the cost of the extra space, is speed: once the key has been hashed, saving or retrieving the element (assuming no collisions) takes $O(1)$ time. With collisions, however, hash tables do have a worst case retrieval runtime (when every element collides) of $O(n)$.

Generally we would like to use hash tables when we want direct access to unsorted data based on a key and there exists a fast-running function for generating the key for each object (assuming the object itself isn't its own key). We would not want to use hash tables when we need to support sorting, when the elements are not well distributed (that is, many elements hash to few locations), or when a common use case is to access blocks of sequential items; since the items are (hopefully) distributed evenly over the memory allocated to the hash table, we no longer benefit from locality of reference.

Real-world application

C# contains a Hashtable class that holds arbitrary objects. Each object that is added to a Hashtable must implement GetHashCode() to return an int32 that can be used to hash the object. Dictionary<TKey, TValue> provides the same functionality, but restricts objects to being of type TValue, which (assuming TValue is not set to Object) allows the programmer to avoid boxing and unboxing the stored elements. Internally, both use a hash table data structure but different collision avoidance techniques. Hashtable uses rehashing (looking for another location if the first one is taken), while Dictionary uses chaining (multiple items with the same hash are simply added to the bucket for that location).

2.6 Sets and posets

A *set* is an unordered collection of unique items. We define three core operations on sets, each of which takes two sets as input and returns another set as its output.

Union(S,T) is a set containing every element that belongs to at least one of S and T, and is generally written as S ∪ T.

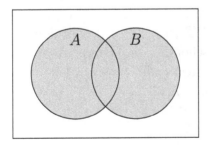

Figure 2.4: The union of
A and B

Intersection(S,T) is the set of those elements contained in both S and T, written as S ∩ T.

Difference(S,T), written S - T, is every element contained in S but not in T.

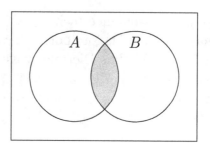

Figure 2.5: The
intersection of A and B.

Finally, we have one additional operation which returns a boolean: subset(S,T) is true if S is a subset of
T (that is, every element in S is also an element of T).
If S is a subset of T and is not equal to T, then it is a
proper subset. We write S ⊆ T (S is a subset of T), S ⊄
T (S is not a subset of T), S ⊂ T (S is a proper subset of
T), and S ⊄ T (S is not a proper subset of T). If S ⊆ T
and T ⊆ S, then S = T. There are additional operations
that apply specifically to sets of strings; we cover these
in subsection 13.2.2.

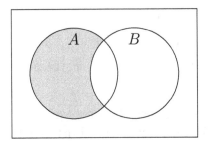

Figure 2.6: The
difference between A and
B (that is, A-B)

There are several variations on sets. A multiset is a
set which allows duplicates, either storing multiple copies
of the same value or simply keeping a count of how many
times that value exists in the set.

A *poset*, or partially ordered set, is a set in which
we do impose an ordering among some elements. This
means that for some binary operation[13] ≤ and elements
b and c, it may be the case that b≤c, it might be the
case that c≤b, or b and c may have no relationship.

When all elements in the set are related by operation
≤, meaning that for any two elements f and g in the set
either f≤g or g≤f, then ≤ imposes a total order. For
example, the standard less than or equal operation is a
total order on the set of real numbers; given any two
numbers, either they are the same or one is larger than
the other.

We require that the relation be reflexive (every ele-

---

[13]A binary operation is one that acts on two operands; for example, the plus operation is used to find the sum of two values.

{4, 7, 2, 16, 1004}   {3, 3, 6, 3, 9}

Figure 2.7: A set of   Figure 2.8: A muiltiset
     integers   of integers

ment in the set is less than or equal to itself), antisymmetric (it cannot be true that both b is less than or equal to c AND c is less than or equal to b, unless b=c) and transitive (if b is less than or equal to c, which is less than or equal to d, then b is less than or equal to d).

Notice that a heap is a partially ordered multiset; it may have multiple copies of the same value and each value has a defined relationship only with its parent and children.

Real-World Example

Let $\leq$ be the relationship "is a decendant of", where we define that every person is a decendant of himself. Then the relationship is antisymmetric (if I am your decendant then you cannot also be descended from me) and transitive (if I am descended from you and you are descended from grandpa, then I am also descended from grandpa). It is a partial rather than a total ordering because it is possible that neither you nor I is a decendant of the other.

Real-World Application

Relational databases[a] contain tables that store sets of rows. An ordering can be imposed when

34

data is displayed (in SQL, we do this with the
ORDER BY keyword), but no such restriction
is imposed on the actual saved data and thus it
can not be assumed that rows in the database
are stored in any particular order.

---

^aA relational database is structured according to the
relationships between stored items. We cover relational
and hierarchical databases in chapter 30.

2.7 Specialized data structures

Later in the book we cover more specialized data structures. Chapter 5 describes some common data structures
on graphs (which are formally introduced in chapter 4).
Chapter 32 introduces the concept of amortized runtime
(where we care about the total time taken over a series
of operations rather than the time for any individual operation) and chapter 33 describes a data structure that
we analyze using amortized runtime.

Chapter 3

Classes of problems

Computer scientists classify problems according to how long they take to solve, relative to the size of the input. By classifying a problem in this way, we determine how difficult it is to solve. In practice, this allows us to avoid spending time on problems that cannot be solved quickly enough for the answer to be useful.

The easiest problems, in the class P, can be solved in polynomial time. This is any problem that has a solution whose runtime is the size of the input raised to some constant. We think of these as being the problems which have efficient solutions. This class includes many well-known problems such as sorting a list. Problems in this class are also called tractable. In general, if you can show that a problem is in P, then you can solve it in a reasonable amount of time.

The set P is a proper subset of the set EXP of problems which can be solved in exponential time; any problem which can be solved in $O(n^2)$ time can naturally also be solved in $O(2^n)$ time.

Math Alert - Lookback to Chapter 2

Given two sets A and B, A is a subset of B and B is a superset of A if every element of A is also an element of B. We write $A \subseteq B$ and $B \supseteq A$.

If B contains everything that A contains and also contains something else, then B is a proper superset of A and A is a proper subset of B. We write $A \subset B$ and $B \supset A$.

For example, the set $\{1,2,3\}$ is a proper subset of the set $\{1,2,3,4,5\}$.

But **EXP** contains more classes than just **P**. The next class up is Nondeterministic Polynomial, or **NP**. A problem is in **NP** if it can be nondeterministically[1] solved in polynomial time. In other words, there is an algorithm that solves the problem by making a series of decisions, and at each decision point it randomly (and luckily) picks the correct choice. So long as there is some series of steps that lead to the answer, the algorithm happens to pick the correct steps. Another (more useful) way of saying this is that a problem is in **NP** if its solution can be checked (deterministically - that is, following a predefined sequence of steps) in polynomial time. **NP** is a superset of **P**; any solution that can be found in polynomial time can also be checked in polynomial time.

One of the great open questions of computer science

---

[1]A deterministic algorithm, given an input, will run through the same sequence of states and return the same output every time. Mathematically, it maps a domain of problem instances to a range of solutions. A nondeterministic algorithm can exhibit different behaviors for the same input.

is whether **NP** is a proper superset of **P**; in other words, are there problems that are in **NP** but not in **P**, or are these the same set? Another way of asking this is, can every problem whose solution can be quickly verified by a computer also be quickly solved by a computer? Most computer scientists believe that $P \neq NP$, but no mathematical proof has ever been found[2].

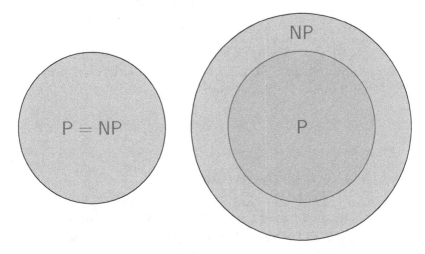

Figure 3.1: The $P \overset{?}{=} NP$ Problem: Are they the same set (left) or is **P** a proper subset of **NP** (right)?

For example, consider the partition problem. The problem is, given a multiset (a set that can have repeated values) of positive integers, determine whether it can be partitioned into two subsets such that the sum of the numbers in the first set equals the sum of the numbers

---

[2]The question of whether $P = NP$ is one of the seven Millennium Prize Problems - important mathematical questions which have resisted solution and for which a prize of $1 million apiece has been established for a proof.

in the second set. If the multiset is partitioned into two subsets {S1,S2}, it is trivial to add up the values in each set and determine whether the two sums are identical, but actually determining which values to put in each set (assuming $P \neq NP$) cannot be done in polynomial time.

$$S = \{1,1,2,3,4,5,6\}$$
$$S_1 = \{1,1,2,3,4\}$$
$$S_2 = \{5,6\}$$

Figure 3.2: A simple example of the partition problem. The multiset {1,1,2,3,4,5,6} can be divided into the multisets {1,1,2,3,4} and {5,6}, each of which sums to 11.

Down in the Weeds

In the paragraph above, we said that the partition problem cannot be solved in polynomial time, provided that $P \neq NP$. This is true only if we note an important distinction between the value and size of the input.

The difficulty of a problem often depends on how the input is encoded. Technically speaking, a problem is in P if it can be solved by an algorithm which runs in time polynomial in the length of the input - that is, the number of bits required to represent the input. It runs in pseudo-polynomial time if it is polynomial in the numeric value of the input, which is exponential in its length. For example, consider a problem instance with an input of one billion and an algorithm which requires n operations. If n is the number of digits required to represent the number (10 in this case, assuming base 10), then the algorithm is polynomial. If n is the value of the input (1,000,000,000), then the algorithm is pseudo-polynomial. In the latter case, the number of operations required grows much more quickly than the number of bits of input.

Some problems in NP are called NP-hard; an NP-hard problem is (somewhat recursively) defined as any problem that is at least as hard as the hardest problem in NP. To understand what this means, we must first consider the principle of reduction.

A problem B can be reduced to a problem C if a solution to problem C would also let us solve problem B in polynomial time. In other words, if we have an oracle which provides the answer to problem C, we can (in polynomial time) change that into an answer to problem B. A decision problem is NP-hard if every problem in NP can be reduced to it, which is to say that finding an efficient solution to the problem would also result in an efficient solution to every problem in NP.

Notice that a problem does not have to belong to NP in order to be NP-hard; it only has to be at least as hard as everything that is in NP. This means that some NP-hard problems (which are not in NP) may be much harder than other problems which do belong to NP.

A problem which is both NP-hard and a member of NP is known as NP-complete. Because every NP-complete problem can be reduced to every other NP-complete problem, reducing any NP-complete problem to a new problem and demonstrating that the new problem belongs to NP is sufficient to prove it to be NP-complete.

Down in the weeds

If an NP-complete problem has a pseudo-polynomial solution, we say that it is weakly NP-complete. If it does not (unless $P = NP$) then it is strongly NP-complete.

To resolve the question of whether $P = NP$ would require that we either give an algorithm which solves an NP-complete problem in (deterministic) polynomial time (in which case $P = NP$), or prove that no possible algorithm can accomplish this (in which case $P \neq NP$).

Advanced topic: NP-complete reduction
Suppose we have the following problems:

Subset sum Given a multiset S of integers and a value w, is there a non-empty subset of S that sums to w?

Partition Given a multiset S of integers, can S be partitioned into two subsets S_1 and S_2 whose sums are equal?

Given that Subset sum is NP-complete, we can show that Partition is also NP-complete as follows.

1. The first step is to show that Partition is in NP. Given two subsets S_1 and S_2, we can

find the sum of the contents of each set and compare them in time proportional to the total number of values. Since the solution can be checked in linear (thus, polynomial) time, the problem belongs to the class NP.

2. The second step is to show that Partition is NP-hard. We do this by showing that a polynomial-time solution to the new problem would also give us a polynomial-time solution to a problem we already know to be NP-hard, so Partition is at least as hard as that problem.

   Suppose we have a polynomial-time algorithm that solves Partition, and a Subset sum problem we would like to solve. We have the set S and would like to know if there is a subset with total value w. This is equivalent to asking whether we can break S with sum $|S|$ into a multiset S_1 that sums to w and a multiset S_2 that sums to $w_2 = |S|-w$.

   Let x be the difference between w_1 and w_2 and add it to S, then run the Partition algorithm on the new set. If the problem is solvable, it will return two partitions with the same sum, which is half of $|S|+x$. Due to how we chose x, removing it now gives the sets S_1 and S_2, one of which is the solution to the original Subset sum problem. The additional work took linear time, so we

43

have a polynomial-time solution for Subset sum.

Example

$S = \{5, 10, 10, 30, 45\}$, $w = 25$

$|S| = 100$, $w_2 = 100 - 25 = 75$, $x = 75 - 25 = 50$

$S_a = \{5, 10, 10, 30, 45, 50\}$

$S_1 = \{5, 10, 10, 50\}$

$S_2 = \{30, 45\}$

Solution: $\{5, 10, 10\}$

This shows that Partition is NP-complete and a polynomial-time solution for it would be a proof that P=NP.

There are a number of additional complexity classes, but the two discussed in this section are the most well-known. The others tend to be defined in terms of Turing machines, which will be covered later in this book.

Further reading

Some common NP-complete problems will be discussed in appendix B. For more about classes of problems, see Chapter 13 on languages and Chapter 14 on Turing machines.

Part II

Graphs and Graph Algorithms

Chapter 4

Introduction to Graph Theory

4.1 The seven bridges of Königsberg

It is, I believe, a requirement that every introduction to graph theory should start by describing the Königsberg bridge problem. This problem is important not for its own applications, but because it was the start of a new field: graph theory.

The town of Königsberg (now Kalingrad) had a river flowing through it; the river divided the city into four regions, which were connected by seven bridges. The question arose of whether it might be possible to take a walk through the city, crossing every bridge exactly once.

The problem was eventually brought to the attention of the mathematician Leonard Euler, who declared it trivial but found it nevertheless caught his attention, as

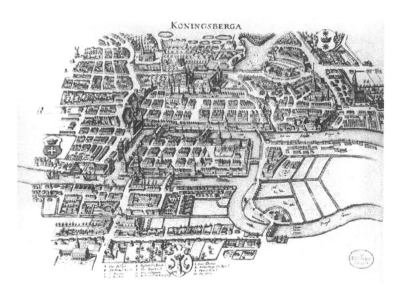

Figure 4.1: Public domain map of Königsberg by
Merian-Erben, 1652.

no existing branch of mathematics was sufficient to solve
it. The key realization is that topological deformations
are not important to the solution; that is, changing the
size and shape of the various parts does not change the
problem, provided that the connections do not change[1].

Thus, we can simplify the map in figure 4.1 by replacing each region with a vertex and each bridge with
an edge between two vertices. That gives us the graph
in figure 4.2.

The key logical insight[2] is that to enter and then leave

---

[1]Euler called this "geometry of position".

[2]*Solutio Problematis ad Geometriam Situs Pertinentis*, Com-
mentarii academiae scientiarum Petropolitanae 8, 1741, pp. 128-
140. English translation available in Biggs, Lloyd & Wilson's
"Graph Theory 1736-1936."

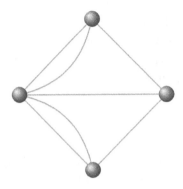

Figure 4.2: The bridges of Königsberg, as a graph.
Notice that each vertex has odd degree, meaning that it
has an odd number of edges touching it.

a landmass requires two separate bridges, so any landmass which is not the starting or ending position must be
the endpoint of an even number of bridges. In the case of
Königsberg, all four regions contained an odd number of
bridges, making the problem insolvable. A path through
a graph which visits every edge exactly once is now called
an Eulerian path.

4.2 Motivation

Graphs are extremely important in computer science because so many problems can be represented as graphs. In
the case of the Königsberg bridges, turning the city into
a graph allows us to ignore the unimportant details (the
actual geography of the city) and focus on the important part (the connections between the various parts of
the city). In many cases, reducing a problem statement
to an equivalent problem on a particular class of graph

gives us useful information about how difficult that problem will be to solve. Certain problems are **NP**-hard on arbitrary graphs, but have efficient - often $O(n)$ - solutions on graphs that have certain properties.

In this chapter and the chapters that follow, you'll learn the vocabulary associated with graphs and some common data structures that use graphs. We'll see how to represent graphs both visually and in formats more convenient for computing. After that, we'll cover well-known graph algorithms and some of the common graph classes. By the time you finish Part II, you should be able to recognize where to apply graphing techniques to problems of your own.

Definition

A graph class is a (usually infinite) collection of graphs which can be defined by a particular property; whether or not a given graph has this property determines whether it is a member of the class.

Example

Bipartite graphs are graphs where the vertices can be partitioned into two sets such that every edge goes between a vertex in one set and a vertex in the other set.

4.3 Terminology

A graph is a way of representing relationships in a set of data. Graphs are often drawn with circles for vertices and lines between the circles representing edges, but we'll see other ways to represent them as well. Two vertices are called adjacent if there is an edge between them, and non-adjacent if there is no edge between them.

Vertices in a graph are also known as nodes; the two terms are largely used interchangeably. However, the point on a polygon where two or more edges meet is always a vertex, and a piece of memory which holds both a vertex and its collection of edges is always a node.

4.3.1 Parts of graphs

We often refer to a subgraph or induced subgraph of a graph. A *subgraph* of a graph is simply any number of the vertices of the graph, along with any number of edges (that also exist in the original graph) between those vertices. An *induced subgraph* is any subset of the vertices, along with every edge of the graph that connects two of those vertices.

A *proper* subset of a set contains less than all of the original set; in other words, a proper subset of the vertices of the graph will contain fewer vertices than the original graph, while a regular subset could be the entire vertex set.

4.3.2 Graphs with all edges or no edges

A *complete* (sub)graph, or *clique*, is one that contains every possible edge between its vertices. An *indepen-*

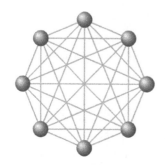

Figure 4.3: K_8, the complete graph on eight vertices.

Figure 4.4: A disconnected graph with six connected components of size 1.

dent set (or *stable set*) is a set of vertices with no edges between them. Figure 4.3 shows K_8; in graph theory, the letter K with an integer subscript means a complete graph on that many vertices.

A graph or subgraph in which there is a path from any vertex to any other vertex is called *connected*; a graph that is not connected is made up of multiple connected components[3].

Given a graph G, its complement G' is another graph on the same vertices; for any pair of vertices, G' has an edge between them if and only if G does not. In figure 4.4, we see the graph which is the complement of K_6; rather than containing every possible edge, it has none of them.

---

[3]A connected component of a graph is a maximally connected subgraph. In other words, a set of vertices in the graph such that there is a path from any vertex in the set to any other vertex in the set and such that no vertex in the set has an edge to any vertex outside the set.

Math Alert

The prime symbol ($\prime$) is used in mathematics to represent an object which is derived from another object. In this case we are using it for the graph G' which we obtain from G by removing all of the edges and putting edges where none previously existed. This is similar to its use in set theory to denote the complement of a set[a].

When we discuss languages in Chapter 13, we will use an alternative notation, denoting the complement of a language A as $\overline{A}$. This notation (also in common use) makes it easier to deal with complements of complements.

---

[a]In calculus, the prime symbol is commonly used to indicate the derivative of a function, which has nothing to do with complements. The meaning of this symbol varies wildly depending on context!

4.3.3 Loops and multigraphs

We generally work with simple graphs, which are graphs that do not contain loops (an edge from a vertex back to itself) or multiple edges (more than one edge between two vertices); when we say graph without specifying otherwise, we always mean a simple graph. A graph with loops can be called a nonsimple graph, and one with multiple edges is a multigraph. For the rest of this book, when you see the word graph, assume that it means a simple undirected[4] graph unless noted.

---

[4]We will discuss directed graphs in section 4.5.

4.4 Representing graphs

When discussing the size of a graph, we commonly use n for the number of vertices and m for the number of edges[5]. In figure 4.3, we have $n=8$ and $m=28$; in figure 4.4, $n=6$ and $m=0$. The amount of space the graph requires will depend on how we store it; common methods include adjacency lists and adjacency matrices.

4.4.1 Representing graphs with adjacency lists

When using an adjacency list representation, each vertex of the graph is stored with a list of the vertices to which it is adjacent. When this is implemented with a set of linked lists, we have a space requirement of $O(n+m)$[6]. For a *sparse* graph (one with very few edges), this reduces to $O(n)$. For a *dense* graph (a graph with many edges, such as the complete and near-complete graphs) this reduces to $O(n^2)$.

4.4.2 Representing graphs with adjacency matrices

The other common way to store a graph is as an adjacency matrix, which is a matrix with the following prop-

---

[5]It is common to use V for the set of vertices and E for the set of edges, so $|V| = n$ and $|E| = m$; that is, n is the size of V and m is the size of E.

[6]We have n linked lists, some of which may be empty (if the graph is disconnected). Each undirected edge appears on two lists, so the total number of nodes on the lists is $2m$. This gives a total of $O(n+m)$ space.

A: BCDEFGH
B: ACDEFGH
C: ABDEFGH
D: ABCEFGH
E: ABCDFGH
F: ABCDEGH
G: ABCDEFH
H: ABCDEFG

Figure 4.5:
Adjacency list
representation of
figure 4.3.

A:
B:
C:
D:
E:
F:

Figure 4.6:
Adjacency list
representation of
figure 4.4.

erties:

- Every cell in the matrix is either 0 or 1.

- The cell at position (i,j) is a 1 if and only if there exists an edge between vertices i and j. This is also true of the cell at position (j,i).

- As a result of the fact above, the number of 1s in the matrix is double the number of edges in the graph.

- The diagonal is always zero, because no vertex has an edge to itself[7].

---

[7]The diagonal of a matrix is those cells where the column is the same as the row; that is, those in positions (0,0), (1,1), etc. See figure 4.7 for an example of a matrix that has zeroes only on the diagonal.

$$\begin{bmatrix} 0 & 1 & 1 & 1 & 1 & 1 & 1 & 1 \\ 1 & 0 & 1 & 1 & 1 & 1 & 1 & 1 \\ 1 & 1 & 0 & 1 & 1 & 1 & 1 & 1 \\ 1 & 1 & 1 & 0 & 1 & 1 & 1 & 1 \\ 1 & 1 & 1 & 1 & 0 & 1 & 1 & 1 \\ 1 & 1 & 1 & 1 & 1 & 0 & 1 & 1 \\ 1 & 1 & 1 & 1 & 1 & 1 & 0 & 1 \\ 1 & 1 & 1 & 1 & 1 & 1 & 1 & 0 \end{bmatrix}$$

Figure 4.7:
Adjacency matrix
representation of
figure 4.3.

$$\begin{bmatrix} 0 & 0 & 0 & 0 & 0 & 0 \\ 0 & 0 & 0 & 0 & 0 & 0 \\ 0 & 0 & 0 & 0 & 0 & 0 \\ 0 & 0 & 0 & 0 & 0 & 0 \\ 0 & 0 & 0 & 0 & 0 & 0 \\ 0 & 0 & 0 & 0 & 0 & 0 \end{bmatrix}$$

Figure 4.8:
Adjacency matrix
representation of
figure 4.4.

- The matrix has n rows and n columns, so it takes n^2 space. For a dense graph, this is still linear in the size of the matrix[8].

In a multigraph with loops, not all of these conditions hold true. Specifically, values can be greater than 1 (because there can be multiple edges between two vertices) and the diagonal can be nonzero (because there can be loops from a vertex to itself).

---

[8]The size of the matrix is the sum of the number of vertices (n) and the number of edges (m), but for a dense graph, $m=O(n^2)$.

4.4.3 Representing graphs in memory

When working with a graph in memory, it will often be stored as a collection of nodes. Each node represents a vertex and contains a collection of pointers to other nodes representing the edges to other vertices.

4.4.4 Choosing representations

Which representation of the graph to choose will depend on how dense the graph is and how you plan to use it. For a sparse graph, an adjacency list is much more space efficient than an adjacency matrix as we don't need to store $O(n^2)$ 0s, and it's easy to iterate over all of the existing edges. Additionally, when the graph is dynamic (changes over time), it's easier to add and remove vertices from the adjacency list.

On the other hand, accessing edges is more efficient with an adjacency matrix; determining whether vertices i and j are adjacent requires simply checking whether $A[i][j]=1$, rather than scanning through a list, which can take up to $O(n)$ time. Thus, not only are lookups faster with an adjacency matrix, but the amount of time taken is constant, making them a better choice for applications where predictability is highly desired[9].

---

[9]In real-time applications, we may be willing to sacrifice some performance in order to obtain tighter bounds on the maximum amount of time an operation can require.

4.5 Directed and undirected graphs

In the Königsberg Bridge Problem, all edges of the graph were *undirected*; if you could walk across a bridge in one direction, you could also walk across it going the other way. Graphs where this is true are called undirected graphs, or just graphs, and represent situations where if A relates to B, B must also relate to A. For example, if Alice is Bob's cousin, then Bob must also be Alice's cousin.

In a *directed* graph, or *digraph*, each arrow has a direction showing which way the relationship goes. If Alice likes to spend time with Bob, and we represent this with an arrow from A to B, this doesn't tell us whether Bob likes to spend time with Alice. If he does, then we also have an arrow from B to A. The digraph is *symmetric* if for every directed edge there is an edge between the same two vertices going in the opposite direction. This is equivalent to an undirected graph with just one edge between each pair of vertices that has a pair of directed edges between them, so the graphs can be thought of as being a special case of the digraphs.

At the other extreme, it's possible that there can only be one directed edge between any two vertices; this is an *oriented* or *antisymmetric* graph. For example, if Alice is Bob's parent, then Bob cannot also be Alice's parent (at least, not in any way that's socially acceptable). Taking an undirected graph and orienting every edge (that is, making it a directed edge) results in an oriented graph.

4.6 Cyclic and acyclic graphs

One way to classify graphs is by whether they are *cyclic* or *acyclic*. An acyclic graph has at most one path between any two vertices; that is, there is no path a-b-c-a, where {a,b,c} are distinct vertices[10]. A cyclic graph has at least one cycle: it is possible to find a path that begins and ends at the same vertex. In the case of directed graphs, we add the condition that all edges of a cycle must have the same orientation, clockwise or counterclockwise; in other words, in a cyclic digraph we can find a path from a vertex back to itself by following the direction of the arrows. When programming graph algorithms, care must be taken to handle cycles or the program can fall into an infinite loop.

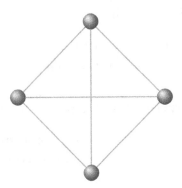

Figure 4.9: Every complete graph is also a cycle.

---

[10]In this case, *c* could also be more than one vertex - we could have a cycle a-b-c-d-e-f-g-h-a. Note that each edge can only be used once - taking a path a-b-c and then going back over the same edges does not give us a cycle!

4.6.1 Trees

Many important algorithms in graph theory operate on *trees*. A tree is simply a connected graph in which there are no cycles. It is usually convenient for us to pick up a tree by its root; we denote one particular vertex to be the root of the tree and define the rest of the vertices by their relationship to the root. Equivalent definitions for a tree are:

- An acyclic graph where a *simple* (without repeated vertices) cycle will be formed if any edge is added[11]

- A connected graph that will no longer be connected if any edge is removed

- A graph where any two vertices are connected by a unique simple path

A tree node is either an internal node (if it has at least one child) or a leaf (if it does not).

4.6.2 Chordless cycles

In many cases, we're specifically interested in chordless cycles. A *chord* is an edge between two vertices on the cycle that is not itself part of the cycle. A chordless cycle is a cycle on at least four vertices that contains no chords; in other words, it is a cycle where any two vertices of the cycle that have an edge between them are consecutive on the cycle[12].

---

[11]This must be a connected graph; do you see why?

[12]For example, if we have a chordless cycle A-B-C-D-E-A, then A does not have an edge to C or D because it does not immediately precede or follow them in the cycle.

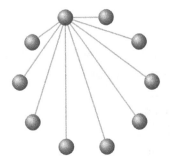

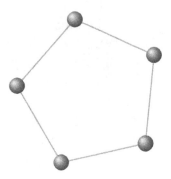

Figure 4.10: A tree with ten vertices. This is a star, which is a tree with exactly one internal node.

Figure 4.11: C_5, the chordless cycle on five vertices.

In chapter 7, we'll discuss several graph classes that are (at least partially) defined by the absence of induced chordless cycles (induced subgraphs that contain cycles with no chords). A graph with no induced chordless cycles is called, perhaps unsurprisingly, a chordal graph.

4.7 Graph coloring

Many problems on graphs involve coloring, which is a way of labeling the vertices (or edges) of the graph. A proper vertex coloring is one in which no adjacent vertices (that is, vertices with an edge between them) have the same color. In other words, it is a partitioning of the vertices into independent sets.

> **Math Alert**
>
> When we talk about finding a coloring of a graph, this doesn't mean we have to be using literal colors. Sometimes we do, but the "colors" can just as easily be a set of integers.
>
> Even if we do use actual colors, the computer will still be processing them as a list of integers and then mapping the integers to colors for display.

Similarly, a proper edge coloring is one in which no two edges incident[13] on the same vertex have the same color. Unless otherwise specified, when we talk about a graph coloring we will be referring to a proper vertex coloring.

Early results in graph coloring involved coloring planar graphs[14], in the form of maps. The four color conjecture[15], posed in 1852, states that for any map consisting of only connected regions[16] with borders of finite length, properly coloring the map requires at most four colors.

A "proof" of this statement was given by Alfred Kempe in 1879, and was generally accepted until shown to be incorrect in 1890[17]. The problem was eventually resolved

---

[13]Two edges are called incident if they share a vertex, just as two vertices are called adjacent if they are connected by an edge.

[14]These are graphs that can be drawn such that no edges meet except at a vertex; see section 7.2 for details.

[15]Having been proven, this is now the four color theorem.

[16]The Continental US, Alaska, and Hawai'i would be considered separate regions under this requirement. Actually, Hawai'i would be several regions.

[17]The author's first published research paper concerned a minimal counterexample to Kempe's faulty proof.

with a computer in 1976; we now have quadratic-time algorithms to four-color any map[18]. There is still no known proof that does not require the use of a computer.

While the map-coloring problem was not actually of any particular interest to mapmakers, map-coloring problems in general are theoretically interesting and have practical applications. Sudoku is a form of graph coloring, where the "colors" are the numbers one through nine.

The chromatic number of a graph is the number of different colors required to properly color it. Another expression of the four-color theorem is that the chromatic number of a planar graph is at most four.

Clearly a graph with no edges has a chromatic number of one (every vertex can be the same color). A complete graph on n vertices has a chromatic number of n (every vertex is adjacent to every other vertex, and so they must all be different colors).

Determining whether an arbitrary graph can be two-colored can be done in linear time[19] – simply color one vertex red, then color all of its neighbors blue, then color all of their neighbors that have not yet been colored red, and so on. Stop when either all vertices have been colored, or on finding a vertex with a neighbor of the same color. Three-coloring, on the other hand, is **NP-complete**! Algorithms are known to determine whether a given graph is k-colorable in exponential time. However, knowing that a graph belongs to a particular class[20] often allows us to find a coloring in polynomial time.

---

[18]Equivalently, any planar graph.

[19]That is, time proportional to the number of vertices plus the number of edges.

[20]Such as the perfect graphs, described in section 7.3.

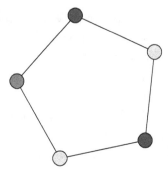

Figure 4.12: C_5, now with a minimal coloring.

Coloring algorithms are commonly used in applications such as scheduling, data mining, networking, etc. For example, consider the problem of assigning times for one-hour meetings, where certain people and equipment are required for multiple meetings. We represent each meeting as a vertex and add an edge between two vertices if they require the same person or equipment. Finding a minimal coloring tells us the number of distinct meeting times required.

4.8   Weighted and unweighted graphs

We can think of the vertices of a graph as being locations and the edges as being paths between those locations, but in reality not all paths have equal length. In an *unweighted* graph, edges simply show which vertices have a direct path between them, but we also have *weighted* graphs, in which each edge is assigned a weight. Usually, but not always, these weights are non-negative integers.

We often refer to the weight as the cost of taking that edge.

What the weight means depends on what the graph represents. In a graph of major cities, the edge weights might be the distance in miles of the shortest highway route between two cities. In a flow diagram, the weights represent the maximum flow through that particular connection.

Chapter 5

Data Structures on Graphs

When designing algorithms, we're often using abstract data structures, in the sense that we know the properties we need the data structure to have rather than the exact data structure being used. A priority queue, for example, is a FIFO (first-in, first-out) data structure where higher-priority elements will jump the line and be served before lower-priority elements. When we actually implement the algorithm, we have to turn that abstract data structure into a real one. The priority queue could, for example, be implemented using a binary search tree or a heap. We previously covered heaps in section 2.4.2, but in this chapter we'll go into more detail on how they are constructed.

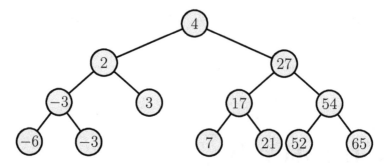

Figure 5.1: A binary search tree.

5.1 Binary search trees

A *binary search tree* (BST) is a rooted binary tree[1] defined recursively as follows: the key of the root is greater than or equal to the key of its left child and less than or equal to the key of its right child (if any), and this is also true for the subtree rooted at every other node.

Operations on a binary search tree take time proportional to the height of the tree, which is the length of the longest chain from the root (which has height zero) to a leaf. This is $\Theta(\lg n)$[2] in the average case[3], but $O(n)$ in the worst case (when each node has one child, making the tree essentially a linked list). Some variations of BSTs

---

[1]A binary tree is one in which each node has at most two children.

[2]Θ means that the runtime is bounded from both above and below; the height of the tree must be at least $\log n$.

[3]Suppose you pick a node at random to be the root. Then on average half of the remaining nodes will go to its left and half will go to its right. Thus, we expect the number of nodes at each level of the tree to be approximately double the number at the previous level, and so we expect to need approximately $\lg n$ levels in the entire tree.

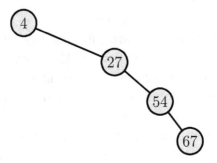

Figure 5.2: An unbalanced binary search tree.
Operations take $O(n)$ time.

guarantee that the height of the tree will be $\Theta(\lg n)$, so
that we can be assured that all operations will complete
in $O(\lg n)$ time.

A BST can be implemented with a collection of linked
nodes, where each node has a key and pointers to its left
and right child and to its parent. Because the nodes are
arranged in such a way that any given node is no smaller
than everything in its left subtree and no larger than
everything in its right subtree, we can print out all the
keys in order by doing an inorder traversal of the tree.

Procedure PrintInOrder(node x)

---

  begin
    if $x \neq null$ **then**
      PrintInOrder(x.left);
      print x.key;
      PrintInOrder(x.right);
    end
  end

Searching a BST is simple: given a pointer to the root and a key we're looking for, we first check to see if the root has our desired key. If the root's key is lower than we're looking for, we recurse on the right child; if it's higher, we recurse on the left child. We stop when either the key matches or the subtree we're attempting to recurse on is null. To find the minimum element, we simply always recurse on the left child, and to find the maximum element we recurse on the right child. In each case, we will examine at most one node at each level of the tree, so the worst-case runtime is proportional to the height of the tree.

How do we create and modify the BST? The first node inserted becomes the root of the tree. To insert any additional nodes, we search for the key value being inserted; when we hit a null pointer, we change it to point to our new node and set the current node as the new node's parent[4].

To delete a node d, we locate it in the tree and then:

- If d has no children, we simply set its parent's child pointer that is currently pointing at it to null.

- If d has one child, that child takes its place.

- If d has two children, we find its predecessor or successor (the nodes which would appear immediately before or after it in an inorder traversal) and again move it up to take d's place (which may then require dealing with that node's children, as if it had been deleted).

---

[4]If the tree is allowed to contain duplicates, then we may hit one or more other nodes with the same key value before finding a null pointer.

5.2 Balanced binary search trees

In order to ensure that operations on the BST take $O(\lg n)$ time rather than $O(n)$ time, we must constrain the height of the tree. When all of the keys are known in advance, we can construct a balanced tree (one where the tree has the minimum possible height). In practice, the elements of the tree often change over time, so we allow the depth to be some amount greater than the minimum possible, while still being $\Theta(\lg n)$.

A self-balancing binary search tree is a BST that automatically keeps its height small (compared to the number of levels required) regardless of any additions or deletions. Self-balancing trees include red-black trees[5], splay trees[6], and treaps.

5.3 Heaps

As discussed in section 2.4.2, a heap is a data structure - specifically, a rooted, nearly complete binary tree - where the key of the root is greater than the key of

---

[5]A red-black tree is a BST where all of the keys are stored in internal nodes and the leaves are null nodes. They have the additional requirements that every node is either red or black, the root and all leaves are black, the children of a red node are black, and every path from a node to a leaf contains the same number of black nodes. As a result of these constraints, the path from the root to the furthest leaf is no more than twice the length of the path from the root to the nearest leaf, because the shortest possible path is all black nodes and the longest possible path is alternating red and black nodes, so no path is more than twice as long as any other.

[6]Splay trees are discussed in detail in chapter 33.

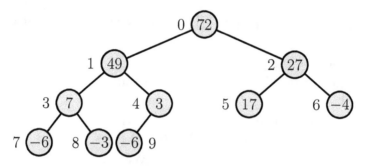

Figure 5.3: A max-heap with nodes labeled by position.

either of its children, and this is recursively true for the subtree rooted at each child[7]. Nearly complete means that the tree is completely filled except possibly on the lowest level, which is filled from left to right.

Suppose we are implementing a heap. Given the heap, number the vertices starting with the root and then going left to right across each level: the root is vertex 0, its left child is vertex 1, its right child is vertex 2, its leftmost grandchild is vertex 3...

Notice that every row contains twice as many nodes as the row above it, which implies that the left child of every node has a label one more than double that of its parent[8]. For any node k, its parent is $\lfloor \frac{k-1}{2} \rfloor$ and its children (if it has them) are $2k+1$ and $2k+2$.

Math Alert
    The L-shaped operators above represent the floor function, which means truncate any frac-

---

[7]Alternatively, the root could be smaller than its children - a min-heap. For consistency we will stick with a max-heap.

[8]Or just double for a 1-based array.

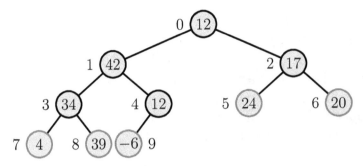

Figure 5.4: In this unsorted binary tree, nodes 5-9 are the roots of heaps of size one.

tion; $\lfloor 2.8 \rfloor = 2$. The inverse function, ceiling, rounds up: $\lceil 2.1 \rceil = 3$

If you prefer to use a 1-based array, then the parent of a node k will be node $\lfloor \frac{k}{2} \rfloor$ and its children will be $2k$ and $2k+1$.

We can do this type of multiplication with bit shifting, which makes determining the position of the parent or child extremely efficient; we then have the location of the desired node if the heap is implemented with an array.

5.3.1 Building a heap

Now that we have defined how the heap is stored in memory, we are ready to build it. A heap is built recursively, building small heaps and combining them to make larger heaps. To start, suppose we have an array A of size n and interpret this as a binary tree, as discussed above. Notice that each leaf of the tree (any item in position $\lfloor \frac{n}{2} \rfloor$ through n-1) is the root of a heap of size 1.

Now consider those internal nodes at the second-lowest

73

level of the tree. If such a node's key is larger than that of either child, it is the root of a max-heap. If not, we swap it with the child that has the larger key so it becomes the root of a max-heap, and then recurse on the new child to ensure that the new subtree retains the heap property. We continue combining heaps in this way until the entire array has been processed.

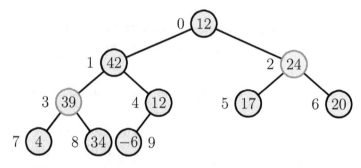

Figure 5.5: Each leaf which is larger than both its parent and its sibling switches places with the parent.

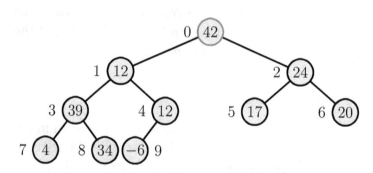

Figure 5.6: Promoting a child may destroy the heap property of the subtree that child was previously the root of. In this case, the new node 1 is smaller than one of its children.

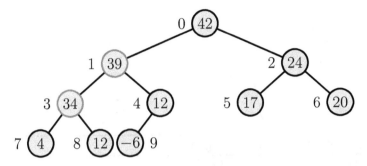

Figure 5.7: Eventually no node has a value larger than that of its parent and the graph satisfies the heap property.

We could represent this process in code as follows. In addition to .length, which as usual is the number of elements in the array, we define .heapSize to be the number of elements in the array that are part of the heap.

Algorithm 1: BuildMaxHeap

Input: Array A
Output: Array A sorted into a max-heap
begin
  | A.heapSize = A.length
  | **for** $i = \left\lceil \frac{A.length}{2} \right\rceil$ *downto 1* **do**
  | | MaxHeapify(A,i)
  | **end**
end

In BuildMaxHeap, we iterate over all of the internal nodes, starting with the lowest. For each selected node, we check to see if it is larger than each of its (up to) two children. If it is, then because each child is already the root of a max-heap, this node is now the root of a new,

Algorithm 2: MaxHeapify

Input: Array A, index i

begin

    left = LeftChild(i)

    right = RightChild(i)

    if *left < A.heapSize and A[left] > A[largest]*
    then

      | largest=left

    else

      | largest=i

    end

    if *right < A.heapSize and A[right] >*
    A[largest] **then**

      | largest=right

    end

    if *largest ≠ i* **then**

      Swap(A[i],A[largest])

      MaxHeapify(A,largest)

    end

end

larger max-heap. If it is not, we swap it with the larger
of its two children; this may cause the subtree rooted at
that child to no longer satisfy the heap property (in the
case that the new element was smaller than not only its
child but also a child of that child, as was the case in
figure 5.5), so we call MaxHeapify again on that subtree.

In the worst case, every time we combine heaps the
new root has to float all the way down to the bottom of
the tree. Each node that is treated in this way may have
to be compared to $O(\lg n)$ descendants, with each comparison taking a constant amount of time. Multiplying
by n nodes gives a total runtime of $O(n \lg n)$.

Algorithm 3: Heapsort

Input: Array A
Output: Sorted array A
begin
    BuildMaxHeap(A)
    for $i = A.length$ *downto 2* **do**
        Swap(A[1],A[i])
        A.heapSize = A.heapSize-1
        MaxHeapify(A,1)
    end
end

In the BuildMaxHeap and MaxHeapify algorithms,
the .heapSize parameter might appear to be redundant.
The check for whether any node is less than A.heapSize
will always return true because we set the heapsize equal
to the size of the array. When running heapsort, however,
it will mark the end of the remaining unsorted elements
of the heap.

In heapsort, after building the heap we move the root (which is the greatest element) to the end of the array, where it will stay. We then decrement heapSize and call MaxHeapify again on the remainder of the array.

Each time heapSize is decremented, the remaining heapsize-1 elements of the array other than the root form a heap and calling Heapify on the root will restore the heap property. The element moved to the end of the array was the largest element remaining, so after the kth iteration the elements in positions [heapsize....n] are the k largest elements in sorted order.

5.3.2 Adding elements to a heap

When adding an element to a heap, it is inserted at the next available location (that is, the first empty spot in the array). If the new element is larger than its parent, adding it destroys the max-heap property. In this case, we need to bubble it up by recursively swapping it with its (smaller) parent. The tree has maximum height O(lg n) and each comparison/swap takes O(1) time, so the total runtime for the insertion is O(lg n).

5.3.3 Removing the root of the heap

To pop an element from the heap, we simply remove the first element of the array; however, this leaves an empty spot in the heap, which we replace with the final element of the heap, leaving a nearly complete tree as required. We then allow the new root to bubble down, swapping it with its larger child until the tree again has the heap property.

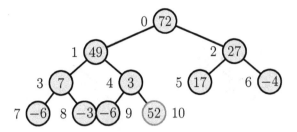

We place the new element (with key 52) in the first open position, which may (and in this case does) invalidate the heap property.

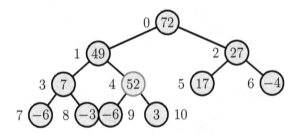

We restore the heap property by bubbling up the new node to its correct position in the heap.

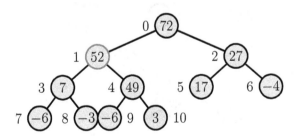

With 52 in the correct position, the heap property has been restored.

Figure 5.8: Adding an element to the heap.

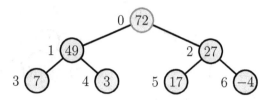

To remove the root, we replace it with the last element from the lowest level of the heap.

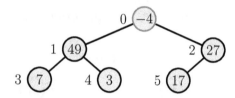

We then bubble the new root down to the correct location in the heap.

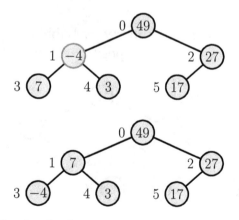

Again the heap property is restored.

Figure 5.9: Removing the root of the heap.

Chapter 6

Well-Known Graph Algorithms

6.1 Introduction

Certain algorithms on graphs come up again and again in various applications, to the point where knowledge of them is simply assumed. Often, these algorithms represent various ways of sorting a graph or finding a subgraph with a particular property. Understanding the relative advantages of these fundamental algorithms is the key to being able to recognize when to use each one in practical applications.

In this chapter, we'll start by explaining breadth-first search (BFS) and depth-first search (DFS), both of which turn an arbitrary graph into a search tree. In each case, we choose a vertex of the graph to be the root of a tree and recursively explore the edges of each vertex until every vertex in the graph[1] has been added to a spanning tree[2]. We'll discuss what types of applications each kind of search tree is useful for. We'll then move on to a discussion of finding shortest paths.

When analyzing the runtime of graph algorithms, there are two different notational systems in common use. One is to denote the number of vertices by n and the number of edges by m. The other is to take the size of the sets of vertices and edges. Given a graph G, we have the set $V(G)$ [read "vertices of G"] and the set $E(G)$ [read "edges of G"], so $n=|V(G)|$ and $m=|E(G)|$.

Math Alert

Recall that in math, surrounding a value with bars means to take the absolute value, or size; here it means the size of the set, so $|V(G)|$ can be read as the size of the set of vertices of G. When G is understood, we may simply refer to the sets V and E.

6.2 Breadth-first search

In breadth-first search, we first explore all vertices which are adjacent to the root. We then explore all vertices adjacent to the root's neighbors that have not already been explored, and so on. In this way, we discover all vertices

---

[1]That is, every vertex that is reachable from the root; this will be all vertices if the graph is connected.

[2]A spanning tree of a graph is a tree which contains all of the vertices of the graph.

that are at distance k from the root (usually denoted s, for source) before finding any vertices at distance $k+1$.

When the algorithm concludes, the depth of each node of the tree is the minimum number of edges (that is, the length of the shortest path) required to get to it from s in both the tree and the original graph. This path can be found by following parent pointers until reaching s.

Algorithm 4: Breadth-first search

Input: An arbitrary graph, with one vertex s chosen as the source and with each vertex having the following properties:

- "distance" (initially set to infinity)

- "parent" (initially set to null)

- "marked" (initially set to false)

Output: A spanning tree for the graph, where each vertex is as close as possible to the source.

begin
    Initialize queue Q
    Set s.distance=0
    Mark s
    Enqueue(s)
    while Q *is not empty* **do**
        Dequeue u
        foreach *vertex* $v \in Adj(u)$ **do**
            if v *is marked* **then**
                continue
            end
            Set v.parent $= u$
            Set v.distance $= u$.distance+1
            Mark v
            Enqueue v
        end
    end
end

What is the runtime of BFS? During initialization, each vertex of the graph has the three mentioned properties initialized, in constant time for each vertex, for a total of $O(n)$. Each vertex is enqueued, dequeued, and has its properties updated at most one time each, all of which are $O(1)$ operations, for another $O(n)$. Finally, we look at every neighbor of every vertex to see if it has been marked yet, which takes another $O(m)$ time. This gives us a total runtime of $O(n+m)$. Storing the graph required $n+m$ space and the queue takes $O(n)$ space, so the space requirement is $O(n+m)$ as well. This also means that BFS runs in linear time relative to the size of the input (which is $n+m$).

6.3 Applications of BFS

As shown above, breadth-first search enables us to find the length of the shortest path from a source vertex s to every other vertex in the graph in linear time. We can then find the actual path by following the parent pointers from the destination node back up to the source, in time proportional to the length of the path. This means that BFS is useful for any number of problems which require finding shortest paths. A few examples follow:

6.3.1 Navigation systems

Consider the problem of getting directions using a GPS. If the mapping system contains the local area as a graph, where vertices are locations (or intersections) and edges are streets (or, more likely, short segments of streets), it can run BFS with your current location as the source.

6.3.2 Testing whether a graph is bipartite

When running BFS, if a vertex ever has an edge to an already-marked vertex whose distance is either the same or is less by a multiple of two, these two vertices will have been given the same color and the graph is not bipartite. Additionally, this edge along with the path or paths to the lowest common ancestor of the two vertices is an odd cycle, which is a certificate that the graph is not bipartite[3]. Bipartite graphs are used in coding theory[4], Petri nets[5], social network analysis, and cloud computing.

6.4 Depth-first search

As in breadth-first search, in depth-first search we start with a source vertex and recursively search the rest of the graph, but now we go as far as we can down one path before exploring any others.

Imagine learning about dogs. A student using BFS might start by looking at the names of all the different dog breeds, from Affenpinscher to Yorkshire Terrier, before going into details. A student using DFS might start with the Affenpinscher, which is a watchdog, so he starts reading about watchdogs, which leads to reading about watches, which leads to the history of time, which leads to... you get the idea. When the search space is exces-

---

[3]A certificate is a proof that the answer returned by a program is correct; see chapter 19 for details.

[4]Coding theory includes cryptography, data compression, and error correction, among other topics.

[5]Petri nets are used to model the behavior of systems.

sively large or even infinite, a modified version of DFS that runs only to a specified depth may be used.

Algorithm 5: Depth First Search

Input: An arbitrary graph, with each vertex having properties "distance" (initially set to zero) and "marked" (initially set to false), and a source vertex s.

Output: A spanning tree for the graph.

begin

    Initialize stack S

    S.Push(s)

    while S is not $empty$ **do**

        $u = $ S.Pop()

        if u is $marked$ **then**

          | continue

        end

        Mark u

        foreach $vertex$ $v \in Adj(u)$ **do**

            if v is $marked$ **then**

              | continue

            end

            Set v.parent $= u$

            S.Push(v)

        end

    end

end

Real-World Application

    I was recently asked for help with a scheduling problem. We had a number of tasks that needed to be completed, with the following restrictions:

1. No task can begin before a certain time.

2. Each task has a maximum amount of time it is allowed to run.

3. A task may have zero or more tasks that it depends on, and zero or more tasks that depend on it; no task may begin until every task it depends on has completed. There are no circular dependencies (so this is a digraph of a partially ordered set).

4. All tasks together may not take more than 24 hours to run.

Shortest path is a common problem, but in this case we actually wanted to find the longest path to each task, which we did using a modification of DFS. This allowed us to impose an ordering on the tasks that guaranteed that at the time any task was processed, every ancestor of that task in the dependency graph had already been processed, so that the latest time required for any parent of a task, plus the amount of time alloted for the task itself, gave us the latest that the task could run. Running the algorithm a second time, in reverse, allowed us to identify any dependency chains that would run past the alloted time, which let us find out which tasks needed to be optimized.

6.5 Shortest paths

Consider the problem of getting from one location to another as quickly as possible. In graph theory, this is the shortest path problem: find the route of least weight between two vertices. In an unweighted graph, this is simply the path requiring the smallest number of edges; in a weighted graph, the path with the lowest total edge weight.

Variations on this problem:

single-source shortest path Find the shortest path from a source node to every other node in the graph. Example: we may want to know the shortest route from the fire station to every location in town.

single-destination shortest path Find the shortest path from every node in the graph to a destination node. This is simply the single-source shortest path problem with all directed edges reversed. We may want to know the shortest path to the ER from any location.

all-pairs shortest path Find the shortest path between every pair of nodes in the graph. Ideally our GPS will be able to find us the best route from anywhere to anywhere.

6.5.1 Dijkstra's Algorithm

Dijkstra's algorithm[6] originally determined the shortest path between two nodes of a graph, but has been expanded so that it now solves the single-source shortest

---

[6]www-m3.ma.tum.de/twiki/pub/MN0506/WebHome/dijkstra.pdf

path problem. It applies to any weighted graph (recall that an unweighted graph is simply a weighted graph where every edge has weight one) where all edge weights are nonnegative.

Algorithm 6: Dijkstra

Input: A graph G and source vertex s.
Output: The distance from s to every other
node in G.
Invariant: S is the set of nodes whose shortest
paths have been determined.
begin
    Initialize vertex set S to null
    Initialize priority queue Q and insert all
    vertices of G
    while *Q is not empty* **do**
        $u = $ Q.ExtractMin()
        $S = S \cup \{u\}$
        foreach *vertex $v \in Adj(u)$* **do**
            Relax(u,v,w)
        end
    end
end

In Dijkstra's algorithm, we start with a source vertex s and a set S of nodes (currently empty) whose distance from s has been determined. We insert all elements of the graph into a priority queue based on their known distance from s; at the beginning, s itself has a distance of zero and every other node has a distance of infinity. We extract the minimum element of the queue, which will initially be s, and relax all of its edges. We continue

---

Algorithm 7: Relax

Input: Adjacent vertices u and v and the weight
w of the edge between them

Output: v.d is the weight of the shortest path
we've found from s to v; if the path
goes through the edge from u to v,
then v.π (the parent of v) is set to u

begin

   if *(v.d > u.d + w(u,v))* **then**

      v.d = u.d + w(u,v)

      v.π = u

   end

end

---

to extract the minimum element and relax its edges until
the queue is empty, at which point every node is labeled
with the length of its shortest path.

Relaxing an edge in this case means that we take the
priority of the current node u, add the distance w to the
new node v, and compare the total to the current priority
of v. If the sum is smaller than the existing value of $v.d$,
we have found a shorter path to v and can replace the old
value; we also mark u as the new parent of v. Any time
a node is extracted from the priority queue, we know we
have already found the shortest path to it because any
shorter path would have to go through the nodes we've
already processed.

This is a greedy algorithm[7], which means that at each
step it does whatever looks best at the time. Because we

---

[7]We discuss greedy algorithms and other approaches to problem solving in part IV.

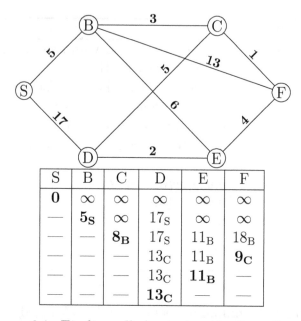

S	B	C	D	E	F
0	∞	∞	∞	∞	∞
—	**5$_\mathrm{S}$**	∞	17$_\mathrm{S}$	∞	∞
—	—	**8$_\mathrm{B}$**	17$_\mathrm{S}$	11$_\mathrm{B}$	18$_\mathrm{B}$
—	—	—	13$_\mathrm{C}$	11$_\mathrm{B}$	9$_\mathrm{C}$
—	—	—	13$_\mathrm{C}$	**11$_\mathrm{B}$**	—
—	—	—	**13$_\mathrm{C}$**	—	—

Figure 6.1: Finding all shortest paths from S using Dijkstra's algorithm. Each row of the table represents one step, in which we process the previously unprocessed vertex of least weight.

maintain the invariant that every node in S is labeled with the length of its shortest path, Dijkstra's algorithm (unlike many greedy algorithms) is guaranteed to return an optimal solution.

Relaxing an edge takes constant time, for a total of $O(m)$ over all edges. Finding the element with the lowest priority to process next takes $O(n)$ time and we do this $O(n)$ times, which gives $O(n^2)$. This adds up to $O(n^2+m)$, where $m \leq n^2$, so the complexity of Dijkstra's algorithm is $O(n^2)$.

Chapter 7

Common Graph Classes

Many problems are quite difficult (NP-hard) on arbitrary graphs, but have efficient (or even trivial) solutions on graphs in a particular class. Inversely, a problem may be known to have no solution on graphs of a particular class. Thus, we can often save ourselves a great deal of trouble if we can demonstrate that a problem instance belongs to a particular class of graphs.

7.1 Forbidden subgraphs

A *forbidden subgraph characterization* of a class of graphs defines a set of structures that may not appear in the graph; the presence or absence of these structures determines whether or not the graph belongs to the class. These forbidden substructures can be defined in a number of ways:

Graphs A graph may belong to a class only if it does not contain any subgraph from a (possibly infinite) set. For example, the bipartite graphs are exactly those which contain no odd cycles.

Induced graphs This is the same as the case above, except that we only care about induced subgraphs (recall that this means some subset of the vertices of the graph, along with all edges between those vertices). For example, chordal graphs are those graphs that do not contain an induced chordless cycle of length at least four.

Homeomorphic graphs Two graphs are homeomorphic if one can be obtained from the other by removing vertices of degree two[1], collapsing the edges into one.

Graph minors A minor for a graph is a subgraph obtained by edge contractions, where an edge contraction happens when we select two adjacent vertices and merge them together.

A class of graphs may have multiple forbidden subgraph characterizations of different types, as we'll see in the next section.

7.2 Planar graphs

In chapter 4, we introduced the Königsberg Bridge Problem, which involved representing a map as a graph. The

---

[1]The degree of a vertex is the number of edges it has, so this means vertices with exactly two edges.

class of graphs that represent maps on a plane (or sphere[2]) has a special name: planar graphs. Formally, a planar graph is one that can be embedded in the plane, meaning that it can be drawn such that no edges intersect except at a vertex. Every map on a plane can be represented by a planar graph: simply replace each region with a vertex and draw an edge through what was previously the shared border.

Kuratowski's Theorem classifies planar graphs in terms of forbidden subgraphs: the planar graphs are exactly those which do not contain a subgraph which is homeomorphic to K_5 (the complete graph on five vertices) or $K_{3,3}$ (the complete bipartite graph on six vertices; see section 7.4).

Consider the following
Suppose you have K_5, which is not planar - there is no way to draw it on the plane without at least one edge crossing. If you add a vertex in the middle of exactly one edge, this doesn't eliminate the crossing, so the new graph is also not planar. This is why the forbidden subgraphs include any graph which is homeomorphic to K_5 or $K_{3,3}$.

Wagner's theorem classifies planar graphs as those that do not contain these same subgraphs as a minor.

Euler's formula states that if a finite, connected graph with v vertices, e edges, and f faces is drawn in the plane

---

[2]A plane is just a sphere with the north pole removed. Sorry, Santa.

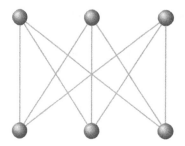

Figure 7.1: $K_{3,3}$, also known as the utility graph.

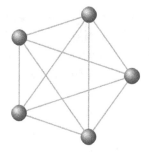

Figure 7.2: K_5, the complete graph on five vertices.

with no edge crossings[3] then v - e + f = 2.

The definition of a planar graph (one that can be drawn in the plane without edge crossings) naturally means these can be nice graphs for display, as it's easier to see where all of the edges go (and in fact every such graph can also be drawn with all edges being straight line segments[4]). A graph drawing application may break a graph into planar components and combine them in order to get a "nicer" visualization. These drawing techniques also have practical applications in fields such as electronic circuit design.

Planar graphs can be broken into smaller pieces by removing $O(\sqrt{n})$ vertices, which helps in devising divide-and-conquer and dynamic programming[5] algorithms on planar graphs.

---

[3]Doing this is, of course, a proof that the graph is planar.
[4]Fáry's theorem.
[5]See chapter 10.

7.3 Perfect graphs

In section 4.7, we introduced the concept of coloring a graph, with a graph's chromatic number being the minimum number of colors required to properly color it. A graph which contains a complete subgraph (an induced subgraph containing every possible edge) of size k clearly must have a chromatic number of at least k. The perfect graphs are those graphs for which this is a tight bound (meaning that the chromatic number is exactly k) and for which this is a tight bound on the chromatic number for every induced subgraph as well. That is, a graph is perfect if and only if it is true that, for both the graph and every induced subgraph, the chromatic number is equal to the size of the largest clique[6].

Perfection is a *hereditary* property, which means that if a graph is perfect, then every induced subgraph is also perfect. The heredity of perfect graphs is clear from the above definition: if every induced subgraph of a graph meets the condition, clearly any induced subgraph of those subgraphs must meet the condition as well.

Perfect graphs actually have multiple equivalent definitions[7]. The strong perfect graph theorem characterizes them as those graphs which contain no odd holes (induced chordless cycles of odd length) or antiholes (the complements of those cycles). The weak perfect graph theorem characterized them as the complements of the perfect graphs (that is, the complement of every perfect

---

[6]Yes, we're using the words "clique" and "complete subgraph" to refer to the same concept. That happens sometimes.

[7]Showing that these definitions are, in fact, equivalent, took a bit of work. For details, see *Algorithmic Graph Theory and Perfect Graphs* by Martin Golumbic.

graph is itself perfect) and follows immediately from the proof of the strong perfect graph theorem. Yet another characterization of perfect graphs is that they are those graphs for which the product of the sizes of the largest clique and largest independent set is equal to or greater than the number of vertices in the graph, and this is also true for every induced subgraph.

Problems that are **NP**-hard on arbitrary graphs but have polynomial-time solutions on the perfect graphs include graph coloring, maximum clique, and maximum independent set. Subclasses of perfect graphs (some of which will be covered in this chapter) include the bipartite graphs (those with chromatic number two), chordal graphs (those with no chordless cycles of length greater than three), comparability graphs (which express a partially ordered set), and subsets of these classes[8]. These subclasses are perfect graphs with additional restrictions, as we'll see in the next section.

7.4   Bipartite graphs

Bipartite graphs are those with chromatic number two, and are included largely to show how easy recognizing a graph class can be. Given a graph, select one vertex from each connected component, assign it the first color, and add it to a queue. Every time a vertex is removed from the queue, look at every one of its neighbors and, if it is not yet colored, assign that neighbor the opposite color and add it to the queue. If ever a vertex has a neighbor

---

[8]These subsets include the interval graphs, which are chordal graphs that can be drawn as a set of intervals on a line, and forests, which are graphs where every connected component is a tree.

the same color, then the graph is not bipartite (and the two vertices form part of an odd cycle); otherwise, we finish with a two-coloring of the graph.

Applications of bipartite graphs include petri nets (which are used to describe distributed systems) and various well-known problems including the stable marriage problem[9] and the assignment problem[10].

7.5   Interval graphs

Interval graphs are those graphs which can be drawn as a set of overlapping line segments along the real line, where each segment represents a vertex and two vertices are adjacent if and only if the corresponding line segments intersect.

Like the perfect graphs of which they are a subclass, interval graphs have multiple characterizations. A forbidden subgraph characterization is given in terms of *asteroidal triples*, which is a set of three vertices in the graph such that for any two, there exists a path between them which avoids the neighborhood of the third. Interval graphs are those graphs which are chordal and contain no asteroidal triples.

Probably the most famous application of interval graphs is in genetic analysis; interval graphs were used to deter-

---

[9]In the stable marriage problem, every person in group A is matched with another person in group B such that there is no match he would prefer that would also prefer him.

[10]In the assignment problem, each agent performs exactly one task (where a task may cost different amounts depending on which agent does it) and the tasks are assigned so as to minimize the total cost.

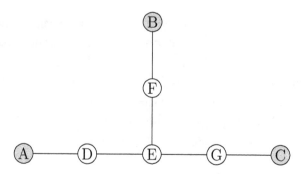

Figure 7.3: Vertices A, B, and C form an asteroidal triple; given any two of these vertices, there is a path between them that does not contain any vertices adjacent to the third.

mine that the subelements of a gene, with high probability, were linked together in a linear arrangement[11].

Interval graphs are commonly used in resource allocation problems, where each interval represents a request for a resource and a coloring of the graph represents an assignment of those resources. For example, if each interval represents a class and two intervals intersect if the classes meet at the same time, then the chromatic number of the graph is the minimum number of classrooms needed and a coloring assigns classes to those rooms.

---

[11]On the topology of the genetic fine structure by Seymour Benzer, *Proceedings of the National Academy of Sciences of the United States of America*, Vol. 45, 1959

Figure 7.4: C_4, the chordless cycle on four vertices, as a circular-arc graph.

7.6 Circular-arc graphs

A superset of the interval graphs[12], circular arc graphs are those that can be drawn as a set of arcs around a circle, such that two vertices are adjacent if and only if the corresponding arcs intersect. If a circular arc graph can be drawn such that part of the circle is not covered, then it is also an interval graph; cutting the circle at the uncovered portion and stretching it out as a line gives an interval representation.

While the interval graphs are a proper subset of both the perfect graphs and the circular arc graphs, the latter classes properly overlap. The class of circular arc graphs contains both graphs that are perfect (the interval graphs, for example) and graphs that are not (the odd chordless cycles). Like the interval graphs, the circular arc graphs can be classified by their forbidden subgraphs.

---

[12]That is, every interval graph is also a circular arc graph. This is a proper superset relation, as the inverse is not true: many circular arc graphs are not interval graphs.

Part III

Non-Graph Algorithms

Chapter 8

Sorting Algorithms

Sorting is a problem most programmers never need to think about; it's simply handled by the language or libraries. In most cases an appropriate sorting algorithm will be automatically chosen based on the size of the input. The .NET framework, for example, sorts arrays using insertion sort, heapsort, or quicksort as needed[1].

So why define your own sort behavior? Perhaps you need a stable sort (that is, one where two items that rank the same will retain the same relative order) and the provided sorts are unstable. Another reason might be that you possess additional information about the data to be sorted, which can allow you to obtain a significant decrease in runtime.

Things that could change what sorting algorithm would be most efficient include knowing that the data:

- Is already close to being sorted.

---

[1]https://msdn.microsoft.com/en-us/library/85y6y2d3(v=vs.110).aspx

- Is in reverse or close to reverse sort order.

- Consists of a finite number of discrete values, where that number is small compared to the number of items to be sorted.

In this chapter, we cover a representative sample of sorting algorithms and their relative advantages and disadvantages.

Most sorting algorithms are comparison sorts, in which two elements of the list to be sorted are compared using some operation which determines that one of them is less than or equal to (sorts before) the other. Comparison sorting algorithms are generally ranked according to the number of comparisons required.

8.1 Small and large sorting algorithms

The first two sorts we'll cover have inefficient average complexities, which means that on large data sets they will be too slow to be practical. On smaller data sets, however, an asymptotically inefficient algorithm can run faster than an asymptotically efficient algorithm.

Given a set of eight items to sort, an $O(n^2)$ algorithm will require on the order of 64 comparisons compared to only 24 for an $O(n \lg n)$ algorithm, but each comparison may require less additional work, resulting in the asymptotically slower algorithm being faster in practice. Sort a thousand items, however, and the 100-fold asymptotic speedup of the more efficient algorithm is less likely to be overcome.

We then cover three comparison algorithms that run in $O(n \lg n)$ average time, followed by two algorithms where we can't count comparisons because we don't actually compare the values to each other.

For a comparison sort, a worst-case runtime of $O(n \lg n)$ is the best we can do, which can be seen as follows. Each comparison determines the relative order of two values and so can be considered as an internal node of a balanced binary tree, where each leaf of the tree is one of the $n!$ possible orderings. A balanced binary tree with k leaves requires $\lg k$ internal nodes or choices (comparisons in this case) on any path from the root to a leaf, so there are $\lg n!$ comparisons made; by Stirling's approximation, $\lg n!$ is $O(n \lg n)$[2,3].

8.2   Sorts for small sets

8.2.1   Bubble sort

Bubble sort is unlikely to be actually useful – it's generally given as an example of a naive sorting algorithm - but makes for a good introduction due to its simplicity. Given an array, compare each pair of adjacent values and swap them if they are out of order.

---

[2]This is simplified somewhat; for a more in-depth explanation with more exact numbers, see chapter 5.3.1 of *The Art of Computer Programming* by Donald Knuth.

[3]Yes, the footnote looks a bit like an exponent here - sorry about that.

Example - Bubble Sort

$$
\begin{array}{c}
3 \\ 1 \\ 4 \\ 2
\end{array}
\rightarrow
\begin{array}{c}
1 \\ 3 \\ 4 \\ 2
\end{array}
\rightarrow
\begin{array}{c}
1 \\ 3 \\ 4 \\ 2
\end{array}
\rightarrow
\begin{array}{c}
1 \\ 3 \\ 2 \\ 4
\end{array}
\tag{8.1}
$$

$$
\begin{array}{c}
1 \\ 3 \\ 2 \\ 4
\end{array}
\rightarrow
\begin{array}{c}
1 \\ 3 \\ 2 \\ 4
\end{array}
\rightarrow
\begin{array}{c}
1 \\ 2 \\ 3 \\ 4
\end{array}
\tag{8.2}
$$

$$
\begin{array}{c}
1 \\ 2 \\ 3 \\ 4
\end{array}
\rightarrow
\begin{array}{c}
1 \\ 2 \\ 3 \\ 4
\end{array}
\tag{8.3}
$$

The kth iteration will ensure that the k largest values are at the end of the list, so after n-1 iterations the list is sorted with a total runtime of $O(n^2)$. Interestingly enough, this is not only the worst-case complexity (which is how we generally measure the efficiency of algorithms) but also the average complexity. The best-case runtime, however, is only $O(n)$. If the list is already sorted or almost sorted, then because bubble sort can detect this (by not performing any value switches), it can run efficiently on such sets. This is a property it shares with insertion sort, which we discuss next. This sort may have been more useful in the days of tape drives, when sequential access was much, much faster than random access.

8.2.2 Insertion sort

Insertion sort is another sort that is simple to implement, but unlike bubble sort it is actually useful in practice for small data sets. It also has the advantage of being intuitive for most people[4].

Insertion sort works iteratively on an array. Given an array of size one, it is clearly in order. For each element added to the end of the array (that is, looking at the next element in the array), either it is larger than all current elements, or it can be moved to the correct place and all sorted elements after it shifted down one spot.

Example - Insertion Sort

$$
\begin{matrix} 3 \\ 4 \\ 1 \\ 2 \end{matrix} \rightarrow \begin{matrix} 3 \\ 4 \\ 1 \\ 2 \end{matrix} \rightarrow \begin{matrix} 1 \\ 3 \\ 4 \\ 2 \end{matrix} \rightarrow \begin{matrix} 1 \\ 2 \\ 3 \\ 4 \end{matrix} \qquad (8.4)
$$

Like bubble sort, insertion sort has a best case complexity (when the array is already sorted) of $O(n)$ and a worst case complexity (when the array is sorted in reverse order) of $O(n^2)$. In practice, the algorithm runs quickly on small arrays and is commonly used to sort small chunks of arrays for recursive algorithms such as quicksort and mergesort[5].

---

[4]Ever play hearts or bridge? If you're like most people you pick up cards one at a time and insert each card into its proper place among the already-sorted cards. That's insertion sort!

[5]After grading papers for a class of 160 students, my practice was to do insertion sort on piles of 8-10 papers, combine those piles using mergesort, then record the grades.

Other nice features of insertion sort are that it is stable, in-place, and *online*. An online algorithm is one in which values can be processed as they become available, rather than the entire input needing to be available at the start.

8.3 Sorts for large sets

8.3.1 Heapsort

Like the previous sorts, heapsort divides the input into a sorted region and an unsorted region and iteratively moves elements to the sorted region. Unlike the previous sorts, heapsort requires some preprocessing. A heap is first built out of the data, and then the largest element of the heap is repeatedly extracted and inserted into the array. Building the heap requires $O(n)$ operations[6]. Extracting the maximum element and rebuilding the heap requires $O(\lg n)$ operations. As we must extract all n elements, this results in a best- and worst-case performance of $O(n \lg n)$[7]. Note that while the best- and worst-case asymptotic complexity is the same, in practice the best-case runtime will be approximately twice as fast[8].

---

[6] $O(n \lg n)$ for some variations.

[7] The Analysis of Heapsort by R. Schaffer and R. Sedgewick. *Journal of Algorithms*, Vol 15 Issue 1, July 1993.

[8] On the Best Case of Heapsort by B. Bollobás, T.I. Fenner, and A.M. Frieze. *Journal of Algorithms*, Vol 20 Issue 2, March 1996.

8.3.2 Mergesort

Mergesort sorts a list recursively: the array is divided into multiple smaller arrays that are sorted, then combined. In a pure mergesort, we can keep dividing until each set contains only one value. We then combine sets; given two sorted sets of size k, we can completely order the combined set in between k and $2k$-1 comparisons.

Example - Mergesort

$$
\begin{array}{ccccccc}
 & & & & 3 & & \\
 & & 3 & 5 & 3 & & \\
3 & 3 & 5 & & 5 & 2 & 1 \\
5 & 5 & & 6 & & 3 & 2 \\
6 & 6 & 6 & & 2 & 5 & 3 \\
2 & 2 & 2 & 2 & 6 & 6 & 4 \\
1 & \rightarrow & \rightarrow & \rightarrow 1 & \rightarrow 1 & \rightarrow 1 & \rightarrow 5 \\
4 & 1 & 1 & & 4 & 4 & 6 \\
8 & 4 & 4 & & & 7 & 7 \\
7 & 8 & 8 & 4 & 7 & 8 & 8 \\
 & 7 & 7 & 8 & 8 & & \\
 & & & 7 & & & \\
\end{array}
$$

(8.5)

This gives us $O(\lg n)$ combined steps that take $O(n)$ time each, for a total runtime of $O(n \lg n)$.

In practice, rather than dividing the sets down to single elements, we stop dividing when the sets are reasonably small and use an algorithm with a better runtime for small sets (such as insertion sort).

8.3.3   Quicksort

Quicksort is interesting in that its worst-case runtime of $O(n^2)$ is worse than that of mergesort and heapsort, but in practice it normally runs 2-3 times faster than those sorts when it hits its average-case runtime of $O(n \lg n)$[9].

Quicksort works by selecting a pivot and arranging all other elements of the array so that all elements to the left of the pivot are less than or equal to that pivot, and all elements to the right are equal or greater. It is then called recursively on the left and right segments of the array, until reaching the base case (in which each segment contains one or zero values).

---

[9]The Algorithm Design Manual by Steven S Skiena

Example - Quicksort

$$
\begin{array}{ccccc}
4 & 4 & 2 & 1 \\
5 & 5 & 1 & 2 \\
7 & 2 & 3 & 3 \\
2 & 1 & 4 & 4 \\
1 & \to 3 & \to 5 & \to 5 \\
3 & 6 & 6 & 6 \\
8 & 7 & 7 & 7 \\
6 & 8 & 8 & 8
\end{array}
\tag{8.6}
$$

The actual number of iterations required varies based on the choice of pivot and the values to be sorted. For example, Lomuto's method is to simply select the final element of the array (or array segment) as the pivot; this is easy to implement, but will result in an $O(n^2)$ runtime when the array is already sorted, because the segment will only shrink by one element with each iteration. This can be avoided by instead choosing as the pivot an element in the middle of the array, a random element, or the median of three random elements. Ideally, the pivot will happen to be the exact median of the data to be sorted, so that the two new partitions each contain half of the remaining data. Given a known (non-random) method for choosing a pivot, a malicious adversary can force $O(n^2)$ runtime by ordering the data such that the pivot will always fall on the same side of every element to which it is compared.

Quicksort will also perform poorly on arrays containing a large number of duplicate values[10], for similar reasons, but this can be fixed by using a three-partition sort (less than, equal, greater than) rather than a two-partition sort. In this case the middle partition doesn't need further sorting, so we can actually obtain faster results when sorting arrays with many duplicates (and if all items are identical we sort in linear time).

Advantages of quicksort over mergesort include sorting in place and a simpler inner loop, allowing it to run faster on most inputs[11]. Disadvantages are the higher worst-case runtime and not being a stable sort[12]; the in-place reordering also doesn't work well if the data is in the form of a linked list rather than an array.

8.4 Non-comparison sorts

As mentioned above, the best worst-case runtime we can obtain for a comparison sort is $O(n \log n)$. Obtaining a better runtime requires that we have additional information (or metadata) about the data to be sorted, in which case it is sometimes possible to improve this to $O(n)$.

In particular, while the number of items to be sorted may be large, there may be a limited number of key values by which those items should be sorted. The following sorts are based on this principle.

---

[10]This is known as the Dutch national flag problem.

[11]*The Algorithm Design Manual* by Steven S Skiena

[12]The reason quicksort is (generally) not stable is that items with the same key may be rearranged during partitioning.

8.4.1 Counting sort

Suppose each of the n items to be sorted has a key which is a positive integer with a value of at most k. We establish an array of length k and loop over all of the items to be sorted, using the array to track the number of appearances of each key (more formally, we are building a histogram of key frequencies).

We now have an array containing the number of times each key appears. Iterate through that array and replace each value with the number of keys that have lower values. After doing this, each cell of the array will contain the correct position for the first element with that key.

Finally, for each element in the input, move that element to the position in the output given by the value in the appropriate cell of the key array, then increment that value by one (so that the next element with this key, if any, will be placed in the next spot of the output).

Example - Counting sort

Consider the following array, where the digit is the key to sort on and the letter is an attached value:

[1a, 3b, 2a, 4c, 1c, 4b, 2a, 2c, 2b, 1b, 3c]

We iterate through the array and find that there are three 1s, four 2s, two 3s, and two 4s. This gives us the histogram [3, 4, 2, 2].

This tells us that the first element with each key should appear at the following positions: [0, 3, 7, 9].

Now iterate through the original array again. The first element is a 1 and will go in position 0.

> The second is a 3 and will go in position 3, and
> so on. Each time we place an element in the out-
> put array we increment the corresponding value
> in the key array. After the first seven elements
> have been placed, for example, the key array has
> changed to [2, 5, 8, 11] and we know that the
> next value, 2c, will go in position 5 in the output
> array.

This entire process requires two loops over the input array (one to fill the key array and one to move elements to the output array) and a loop over the key array to sum the values and determine the final key positions. Additionally, the key array (of size k) and the output array (of size n) must be initialized. The overall runtime is then $O(n+k)$, as is the space usage. If k is small compared to n (for example, a large number of items which are ranked one a scale of 1 to 100), then this is $O(n)$. This is a stable sort.

8.4.2 Radix sort

Radix sort is an older sort[13] that is still useful today; depending on the assumptions, it can be more efficient than the best comparison sorts. The complexity is $O(wn)$ for keys with word size w; when w is a constant, this reduces to $O(n)$. This naturally requires duplication of keys; if each item to be sorted has a unique key, then the key length must be at least $\lg n$[14]. There are several varia-

---

[13]Used by Herman Hollerith for tabulating machines in 1887; he founded one of the companies that eventually became IBM.

[14]Given a base b and a key of length w, the number of different keys is b^w. If w is less than $log_b n$, the number of possible keys is

tions on radix sorting; here we consider least significant digit sorting.

Consider the alphabet the key is drawn from and create one bucket for each letter in that alphabet. For example, if the key is a decimal number, then use ten buckets labeled 0-9. For each item in the list, drop that item into the bucket assigned to the least significant digit of that item's key. For example, if the key is 378, then the item goes into bucket 8. In other words, group the keys based on the last significant digit, but keep their relative order (so that this is a stable sort).

Next group the keys again, but on the second least significant digit; our 378 above is now in bucket 7. And, repeat. Once one pass has been made for each digit in the key, the list is sorted. One way to implement this would be with each bucket represented by a queue; after each pass, the items can be dequeued back to the list.

Why does this work? Consider two keys at the final step of the process. If they have a different most significant digit, the key that should appear first in the sort will appear in an earlier bucket, so they have the correct relative ordering. If the most significant digit is the same, then they will be sorted into the same bucket in the same order in which they were sorted for the previous digit, which by induction will also be correct if that digit is different, and so on. If all digits are the same, then the order doesn't matter (but they will be in the same relative order they started in).

Each item is placed into a bucket (in constant time) once for each character in the key, which gives us our $O(wn)$ time bound.

---

less than the number of items to be sorted.

117

Part IV

Problem-Solving Techniques

Chapter 9

Brute Force or No?

Computer science can be thought of as being how we find ways to solve problems using computers. The work of a computer scientist then boils down to three tasks: determining which problems a computer can solve, telling the computer how to solve them, and predicting how long the process will take.

The choice of which problem-solving technique to use boils down to what attributes of the solution are most important to us. Each algorithm will have some cost to run, which we can generally express in terms of time and space complexity. Time complexity is the amount of time the algorithm takes relative to the size of the input. Space complexity is the amount of memory it requires (again, relative to the size of the input). The *computational complexity* of an algorithm is simply the amount of resources (time and space) required to run it; the computational complexity of a problem is the minimum complexity of any algorithm that could possibly solve it.

However, the resources required to run a program are

not the only costs involved (although they're generally the only ones mentioned in academic papers). We also have to consider the complexity of writing and debugging a program. We might choose to implement a less efficient algorithm when we are willing to give up some speed in exchange for either programmer time (when the faster algorithm will take significantly longer to implement) or accuracy (when the faster algorithm is more likely to have bugs).

Real-world application

I was reviewing a development log a junior developer was working on that was undergoing code review. The reviewer had suggested making a particular change in order to make the code more efficient.

I agreed that the proposed code would be more efficient, but vetoed the change because it would also have made the code more complex. In this case, the code in question was not in a time-sensitive part of the application (the fraction of a second the change might save would never be noticed) and the added complexity would have made it more likely that we'd end up with a bug, either immediately or when the code was updated in the future.

At the extreme end of the efficiency-vs-complexity scale, we have brute force. Brute forcing a problem is simple: iterate through every possible solution and try each one until one of them turns out to be correct. This is most likely to be used when we have a problem that needs to be solved once, and the additional time required to find an efficient solution would be greater than the time savings from running that solution. Of course, sometimes we do brute force simply because we don't know of any better solutions!

For example, if a safe has a ten-digit keypad and you know that the combination is a four-digit number, then absent any other information (and assuming you don't have a limited number of tries) you can find the combination by simply punching in every possible number from 0000 through 9999. This may take a very long time (5,000 tries on average) but the procedure is dead simple. This translates immediately to the digital world: if a website does not enforce strong passwords and does not lock an account after some number of incorrect tries, then given a username we can check every possible password until one of them works.

A brute force solution is often very simple to implement and very difficult to implement incorrectly, making it useful when the problem size is small and accuracy is highly desired.

Chapter 10

Dynamic Programming

10.1 The problem of the missing pieces

Suppose you have an $n \times n$ chessboard, with some missing pieces. How can you find the largest $k \times k$ section of the board with no missing pieces[1]?

If you haven't seen this problem before, take a few minutes to write out a solution and determine the runtime of your algorithm.

When faced with this problem, I reasoned as follows. Each square of the chessboard could belong to many largest sections, but can only be the top left corner of one such. If I label each square with the size of the largest unbroken section it is the top left corner of, the square

---

[1]I was given this problem in an interview with a well-known software company some years ago; quickly providing an efficient solution got me invited to the next round of interviews. Sufficient time has passed that I feel comfortable including the problem here.

with the largest such label marks the section I'm looking for.

Assume that the board is given as an $n \times n$ matrix, where each cell contains a "1" if the corresponding square is present and a "0" if it is not. For each cell, if the current value is 0 then the corresponding square is missing and cannot be part of an unbroken section, so we don't need to update it. If the value is 1, then we can replace it with one more than the minimum value of the three squares below and to the right.

We update each cell of the matrix once, and this involves checking whether the value of the cell is 0, checking the values of up to three additional cells, and setting the cell's new value. Each of these operations is $O(1)$, so the time taken for the entire chessboard is $O(n^2)$.

Notice that this is a linear runtime, not a quadratic one – there are n^2 squares in the chessboard (some of which are missing), so the total time taken by the algorithm is proportional to the number of squares. We could more accurately label this a $\sqrt{n} \times \sqrt{n}$ chessboard[2], which would give us n squares and a total runtime of $O(n)$.

10.2 Working with overlapping subproblems

The approach used here is called dynamic programming. It applies when a problem can be broken up into multiple subproblems, where the solution to a given subproblem will be needed multiple times. This is different from di-

---

[2]Making n the total number of squares and keeping to the usual convention that n is the size of the input.

Algorithm 8: Each cell can have a value greater than 1 only if the starting values of it and the cells to the right, below, and below right of it are 1s.

Input: A matrix M where each cell contains either 1, if the corresponding square is present, or 0, if it is not.

Output: A matrix M where each cell represents the size of the largest board for which the corresponding square is the top left corner.

begin

    for $i=n\text{-}2$ *to* 0 **do**

        for $j=n\text{-}2$ *to* 0 **do**

            if $M[i][j]==0$ **then**

                | continue;

            else

                $M[i][j] = 1 + \min(M[i+1][j],$
                $M[i][j+1], M[i+1][j+1]);$

            end

        end

    end

end

vide and conquer, in which we break up a problem into subproblems that can be solved independently. In my chessboard problem above, each subproblem depended on the solutions for up to three others, and the solutions to all of the the subproblems are saved for later use.

Dynamic programming is generally done by tabulation, as above. This means solving the problem in a bottom-up fashion, where we start with the smallest subproblems and work our way up until we arrive at the answer. Another method is memoization, where we work top down, solving subproblems as they become relevant and caching the results for reuse[3]. Tabulation is the preferred option when we need to solve every subproblem (in my chessboard example, we had to calculate the largest section for each square of the board), due to reduced overhead compared to memoization. When some subproblems in the solution space don't need to be solved, memoization allows us to solve only the subproblems that are actually required.

> **Key Point**
> Where divide and conquer involves dividing a problem into multiple *independent* subproblems, dynamic programming involves dividing it into multiple *overlapping* subproblems. The solution to each subproblem is cached for later reuse.

---

[3]Some people consider dynamic programming to be tabulation only, with memoization being a different technique. Whichever semantics you prefer, the techniques are as described here.

10.3 Dynamic programming & shortest paths

Consider the shortest path problem, in which we have an edge-weighted graph and would like to find the lowest-cost path between two nodes.

> **Definition**
>
> An edge-weighted graph is a graph where there is a cost to taking each edge. The cost of a path from one node to another is the sum of the costs of all edges traversed.

Suppose we have found such a path from s to t that contains another node v. Then the path from s to t must contain a shortest path from s to v, or else we could replace that segment with a shorter path and reduce the length of our shortest path from s to t, a contradiction[4].

> **Key Point**
>
> Dynamic programming (and greedy algorithms) are useful for problems which exhibit optimal substructure; this means that an optimal solution for the problem can be efficiently constructed from optimal solutions to its subproblems. If the fastest way to drive from Madison, WI to Denver, CO is by going through Omaha, NE[a], then this route must also contain the fastest way to get from Madison to Omaha and from Omaha to

---

[4]This is the Bellman principle of optimality.

Denver[b].

When a problem has both optimal substructure and overlapping subproblems, it becomes a candidate for being solved with dynamic programming.

---

[a]This is true, according to Google Maps.

[b]This ignores the fact that Omaha is not actually a single point on the map. In practice, this might not actually be true if, for example, connecting the two shortest paths requires making an illegal left turn.

Shortest path problems provide attractive examples of dynamic programming because the optimal substructure property is intuitive; it seems clear that the fastest way to walk from A to B to C is also the fastest way to walk from A to B and from B to C. Algorithms based on this include Bellman-Ford, which finds the length of the shortest path from a single source to every other vertex in the graph (or from every other vertex in the graph to a single sink) and Floyd-Warshall, which computes the length of the shortest path between every pair of vertices in the graph. In both cases, the idea is that we start with a small subset of nodes which are close to the ones we're interested in and gradually expand the size of this set, using the already-calculated nodes to find the new distances.

Algorithm 9: At the start of the algorithm, $M[s][t]$ represents the length of the edge from s to t, if one exists. Given another vertex i, if the sum of the distance from s to i and from i to t is less than the distance from s to t, then we replace $M[s][t]$ with the new value.

Algorithm: Floyd-Warshall

Input: A matrix M where each cell represents the length of the edge between the corresponding vertices, with 0 on the diagonal and ∞ if no edge exists.

Output: A matrix M where each cell represents the length of the shortest path between the corresponding vertices.

begin
    for $i=1$ to n **do**
        foreach s,t **do**
            $M[\text{s}][\text{t}] = \min(M[s][t], (M[s][i] + M[i][t]);$
        end
    end
end

10.4 Sample applications

10.4.1 Git merge

Another problem commonly used to demonstrate dynamic programming is longest common subsequence, or LCS. The problem is as follows: given two strings A and B, find the longest sequence that appears, in order, in both strings. Letters in the strings are not required to appear contiguously; for example, given A={acdbef} and B={babdef}, {adef} would be a common subsequence.

When merging changes in Git, we find the LCS of the master and working branch. Characters present in the master but not the LCS have been deleted, while characters in the working branch but not the LCS have been added.

10.4.2 LaTeX

This book is typeset in LaTeX, a document preparation system generally used for technical material. One job of the typesetting system is to justify the text; this is done by stretching or compressing spaces between words and characters so that each line is the same length. Another way to justify text is to hyphenate the final word, bumping part of the word to the next line. LaTeX[5] attempts to determine the optimal breakpoints to use such that the overall text is aesthetically pleasing. Failure to do so could mean that several lines in a row must be hyphenated or that the amount of space between words varies

---

[5]Technically, TeX is the typesetting system that's actually doing all the work; LaTeX is built on TeX. But I'm just using LaTeX here for simplicity.

wildly from line to line. LaTeX uses a set of rules to measure the 'badness' of the justification and attempts to find the 'least bad' solution.

Given n possible breakpoints in a paragraph, there are 2^n possible solutions for how to break up the text. The 'badness' of each breakpoint depends on the ones that came before it, meaning we again have overlapping subproblems. Use of dynamic programming techniques brings the runtime down to $O(n^2)$, which can be improved further with additional techniques[6].

---

[6]For details, see *Breaking paragraphs into lines* by Donald E. Knuth and Michael F. Plass, Software: Practice and Experience, vol 11 issue 11, 1981.

Chapter 11

Greedy algorithms

A greedy approach to a problem is one where every time a decision must be made, we choose the one that is locally optimal. In other words, it gives the best solution to the current subproblem even if that wouldn't be the best solution for the overall problem. In the traveling salesman problem mentioned in section 1.6, that meant always going to the closest city that has not yet been visited (that is, choosing the lowest-cost edge that takes us to an unvisited vertex). This is fast (we only have to iterate through the edges incident on the current vertex and find the cheapest) but has no guarantee of finding the best overall solution.

Consider walking around on a plot of land and trying to find the highest point. A greedy algorithm would be to walk uphill as far as you can. Once all directions are downhill, you have found a local maximum - every spot you can immediately walk to is lower than where you currently are. This doesn't mean you've actually found the highest spot available, only the highest spot in your local area (the places you compare to where you're currently standing).

There are some problems for which a greedy algorithm will give the optimal solution; Dijksta's shortest paths algorithm is one example. As with dynamic programming, greedy algorithms work best when the problem has optimal substructure. The difference between the approaches is that dynamic programming is guaranteed to find the solution to an optimal substructure problem because it considers all possible subproblems and combines them to arrive at the optimal solution, whereas a greedy algorithm simply chooses the subproblem that looks best at the time.

For example, consider the problem of getting home from work during rush hour. A greedy approach would be to take whatever route home is least congested close to work; this gets you going faster but risks hitting more traffic closer to home. A dynamic programming algorithm would consider the entire traffic report and choose the route with the lowest overall cost, even if that means the initial road is more congested.

Greedy algorithms tend to be fast, so they are preferred when they are guaranteed to find either the optimal solution to a problem or at least one that's "good enough."

Part V

Complexity Theory

Chapter 12

Understanding Complexity Theory

In chapter 1, we learned how to analyse the runtime of an algorithm so that we can determine the best algorithm to implement for a given problem (or whether a good enough algorithm even exists). In that chapter, it didn't particularly matter what language we used. While we expressed the algorithms in pseudocode, using C#, Java or Python would have given us the same asymptotic runtime.

This isn't to say that programs written in each language would necessarily be equally efficient, but they're all running on the same (theoretical) hardware and using the same data structures, so we expect to see the same growth in runtime as the problem size increases. The underlying assumption is that we have a theoretical computer much like any we might use today, except with an infinite amount of memory (something that, alas, is rarely found in real computers).

One of the roles of complexity theory is determining what computers can and cannot do. In some cases, we may be able to significantly decrease the amount of time required to solve a problem by either using a more efficient algorithm or throwing additional resources (such as processors) at it. Problems which are inherently difficult cannot be solved without significant resources even given an optimal algorithm (the **NP**-complete problems are assumed to be inherently difficult). In some cases a problem may actually be impossible for a particular type of computer to solve, even given unlimited resources.

When we change from one model of computation to another, a problem that was very difficult may become trivial, or a trivial problem may become unsolvable. For example, a quantum algorithm is one that runs on a quantum computer (as opposed to the classical computers that everybody outside of a research lab uses today). There are quantum algorithms that run exponentially faster than the best-known classical algorithms for the same problem, and it has been shown that quantum computers can solve some problems that classical computers will never be able to solve[1].

Background information

A quantum computer is a relatively new model of computation that relies on quantum mechanics. Where classical computers use bits that can be either 0 or 1, quantum computers use *qubits* that exist in a superposition of states - each bit

---

[1]Oracle separation of BQP and PH by Ran Raz and Avishay Tal. *Proceedings of the 51st Annual ACM SIGACT Symposium on Theory of Computing (STOC 2019)*, 2019.

is both 0 and 1 simultaneously. Where a byte expresses one value between 0 and 255, a quantum byte expresses all 256 values at once.

If we then read the qubits, they collapse into a single state - that is, rather than being in every possible state at once, they now have exactly one value. It is not guaranteed that this value will be correct; the algorithm simply manipulates the qubits such that when they are measured, they will collapse to the correct state with high probability.

Going in the other direction, there are models of computation which cannot solve problems which are trivial to solve with today's computers. These models have limitations such as the way in which they can access memory. By demonstrating that a particular problem can be solved using a given model, we put an upper bound on the amount of computing power required to solve it while also giving ourselves access to the tools developed for dealing with that model.

Chapter 13

Languages and State Machines

13.1 Formal languages

A human language, such as English, is a set of letters (in the case of written languages) or sounds (in the case of spoken languages), along with rules for how to combine those letters or sounds to form words and sentences. Similarly, in math and computer science a language is a set of symbols and the rules for combining those symbols.

Languages are classified according to how powerful a computer must be to recognize them. Recognition in this context means that, given a string, the computer can accurately determine whether or not the string belongs to the language. Attributes such as the type of memory available affect the power of the computer and thus the complexity of the languages which can be recognized.

Formally, a language L over an alphabet Σ is the (possibly infinite) set of all legal words which can be formed

143

from that alphabet. For example, we could have the alphabet over $\Sigma = \{a\}$ of $L = a^{2n}$; in other words, all even-length strings consisting only of the letter a. This language would include the strings λ^1 (the empty string - zero is an even number!), aa, aaaa, etc. It is possible for a language to have a finite number of words, an infinite number of words, or even no words at all ($L = \{\varnothing\}^2$).

A class of languages can be defined by the type of machine that can recognize it, the type of grammar that generates it, or in terms of set theory. We'll cover all of these for each class of languages we discuss.

13.2 Regular languages

The regular languages are those languages which can be accepted by *finite state machines*. A finite state machine, or FSM, is a machine which has one start state, one or more accept states, and transitions between those states. To determine whether a string is in the language, you begin at the start state and follow a transition for each letter in the string. If the state reached after the last letter of the string is an accept state, then the string belongs to the language.

In the FSM in figure 13.1, we start at S, which is also an accept state (because we have not seen any letters yet and zero is an even number). When we see one "a" we move to state q_1, and when we see another "a" we move back to S. We continue to follow the edges until we have read in the entire string.

---

[1]This is the greek letter lambda.

[2]This is the null (empty) set, which is not the same thing as the set containing only the empty string ($\{\lambda\}$).

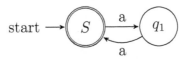

Figure 13.1: A finite state machine which accepts any
string of even length over the alphabet $\Sigma=\{a\}$. The
double circle indicates that S is an accept state.

There are two kinds of finite state machines: deterministic and nondeterministic. In *deterministic finite automata* (DFAs), when the alphabet contains more than
one letter (as most do), each state of the machine must
contain an edge for each letter of the alphabet. Below is
a DFA for the language over $\Sigma=\{a,b\}$ consisting of any
number of "a"s, followed by exactly one "b".

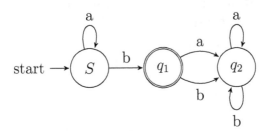

Figure 13.2: A deterministic finite automaton which
accepts strings consisting of any number of "a"s
(including zero), followed by exactly one "b".

State q_2 in figure 13.2 is what we refer to as a dead
state; it is not an accept state and, as following any letter
brings you back to the same place, once you're there you
cannot possibly reach an accept state. In this case, a
string which contains any characters after the one "b" is
not in the language. Notice that because the machine

is deterministic, the transition to take at each step is uniquely determined by the input symbol and current state.

An alternative to the dead state is to use a *nondeterministic finite automaton,* or NFA. An NFA is a finite state machine where a given state may have zero, one, or more than one transition for any given letter. Because we no longer require that every state have a transition for every letter, a dead state is not required. If there is no transition for the next letter in the string, then the string is not in the language.

NFAs are equivalent to DFAs in terms of the languages they can accept. Every DFA is also an NFA (DFAs have to follow the one-transition-per-letter restriction, NFAs are allowed to) and every NFA can be transformed into a corresponding DFA. Figure 13.3 contains an NFA that accepts the same language as the DFA in figure 13.2. We generally prefer to use NFAs over DFAs because they often require many fewer transitions.

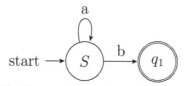

Figure 13.3: A nondeterministic finite automata which accepts strings consisting of any number of "a"s (including zero), followed by exactly one "b".

Suppose we'd like to recognize a slightly more complicated language: the langage consisting of one or more "a"s, followed by zero or more "c"s, zero or more "b"s, and then exactly one "c". We could recognize this lan-

146

guage with the NFA in figure 13.4. Notice that it uses a lambda transition[3] to ensure that the c-loop is not taken again after the b-loop.

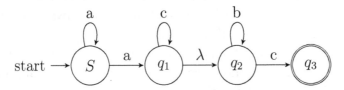

Figure 13.4: An NFA for the language $a^+c^*b^*c$.

What sorts of languages cannot be recognized by finite automata? Notice that these state machines do not have a separate memory, which restricts the length of any comparisons to the number of states in the machine. For example, suppose you wanted to build a machine to recognize the language consisting of any number of matching parentheses, where a right parenthesis always follows the corresponding left parenthesis. You could construct a machine like in figure 13.5.

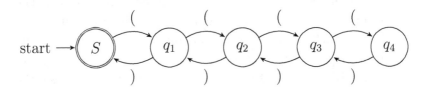

Figure 13.5: A nondeterministic finite automaton which accepts sets of matching parentheses up to a limit of four open sets at a time.

This machine will do exactly what you want, as long

---

[3]A lambda transition allows us to move from one state to another without reading in anything from the input.

as there are never more than four open sets of parentheses
(four left parentheses without matching right parentheses). Exceeding that limit takes us past the ability of
this machine to recognize the string. We can make the
machine larger, adding more states - but always a finite
number of states. If we have $n+1$ states, we can keep
track of up to n transitions, which means that a finite
state machine cannot recognize every string in a language
which makes arbitrarily long comparisons. Later we will
see a method to demonstrate that a given language which
requires such a comparison cannot be recognized by any
finite state machine and thus is not regular.

13.2.1 Regular grammars

A grammar is a set of rules for generating a language.
Where an automata for a language lets you take a string
and check whether or not it belongs to the language, a
grammar allows you to generate any string that is part
of the language. A grammar consists of variables (given
as upper case letters), terminals (the characters in the
alphabet), and transitions converting variables into characters (either variables or terminals). For example, the
grammar in figure 13.6 generates the language shown in
figure 13.5 of sets of parentheses with up to four sets open
at a time.

We use the grammar by starting with S and replacing
a variable at each step until the remaining string consists
entirely of terminals. For example, $S \rightarrow (A \rightarrow ((B \rightarrow (()A \rightarrow (()(B \rightarrow (()()A \rightarrow (()())S \rightarrow (()())$.

This is called a right regular grammar, because in
each production the variable (if one is present) follows
the terminal symbol. Every production rule in a right

148

$$S \rightarrow (A$$
$$S \rightarrow \lambda$$
$$A \rightarrow (B$$
$$A \rightarrow)S$$
$$B \rightarrow (C$$
$$B \rightarrow)A$$
$$C \rightarrow (D$$
$$C \rightarrow)B$$
$$D \rightarrow)C$$

Figure 13.6: A grammar which generates the language of matching parentheses up to a limit of four open sets at a time.

regular grammar takes one of three forms: a variable goes to a terminal, a terminal followed by a variable, or λ. A left regular grammar is identical except that the variable goes to a terminal, a variable followed by a terminal, or λ. Notice that you cannot mix the two; you can construct a left regular or right regular grammar to represent any regular language, but the grammar must be one or the other.

Practical Pitfall

You might expect that a regular expression would be another way to work with regular languages, and from a computer science perspective you would be correct. Regular expressions describe regular languages and have the same expressive power as regular grammars.

In programming, however, regular expressions (regexes) have been extended to handle many languages that are not actually regular, as they involve remembering previous input (backreferences). This makes regexes considerably more powerful than regular expressions in computer science.

But at least theoretical regular expressions are not subject to catastrophic backtracking[a].

---

[a]Catastrophic backtracking occurs when repetition operators (* and +) are nested, allowing the computer to attempt an exponential number of different ways to break apart certain strings and leading (in .NET) to a RegexMatchTimeoutException.

13.2.2 Closure properties

All the words in a language form a set[4]. Sets can be closed under certain operations, which means that if you apply that operation to members of the set, you get another member of the set. For example, the integers are closed under addition, subtraction, and multiplication, because adding, subtracting, or multiplying two integers gives you another integer. They are not closed under division because dividing one integer by another may or may not result in an integer.

Similarly, a class of languages is closed under an operation ∘ if for any languages in the class, applying that operation results in another language in the class. The regular languages are closed under the following operations:

union $A \cup B$ is every word that is in at least

---

[4]Recall that a set is an unordered collection of items.

one of A or B.

intersection A ∩ B is every word that is in both A and B.

concatenation A concatenated with B is the set of words consisting of any string from A followed by any string from B.

complement $\overline{A}$ is every word over A's alphabet Σ which is not in A.

difference A - B is every word that is in A but not in B.

Kleene star A^* is zero or more copies of A.

Kleene plus A^+ is one or more copies of A.

All of these properties are either stated outright or follow logically from the set-theoretic definition of regular languages:

- The empty language $L = \{\varnothing\}$ is regular.

- The language containing only the empty string $L = \lambda$ is regular.

- For each letter in Σ, the language containing only that letter is regular.

- If A and B are regular languages, then A ∪ B, A concatenated with B, and A^* are regular.

No language over Σ which cannot be generated from the above rules is regular.

You can show that the regular languages are closed under a particular operation either by demonstrating that you can create a finite automaton (or regular expression) that represents the closure operation or through combining already-proven closure operations.

Example

Concatenation If A and B are regular languages, adding a λ transition from every accept state of the NFA for A to the start state of the NFA for B^a gives an NFA for A concatenated with B.

Complement Given a DFA for a language L, changing every accept state into a non-accept state (and vice versa) results in a DFA for the complement of L.

Intersection The intersection of the sets A and B (the things found in both) is equal to everything which is not in the set of things missing from A or the set of things missing from B - that is, $\overline{\overline{A} \cup \overline{B}}$ - so knowing that regular languages are closed under union and complement proves that they are also closed under intersection.

---

^{a}and making those states in A no longer be accept states

13.2.3 Pumping lemma for regular languages

To show that a language is regular, I give either a finite automata or a regular grammar that accepts it. How do I show that it is not regular? Failure to find an appropriate machine or grammar isn't proof - perhaps one exists that I simply couldn't figure out.

Instead, to prove a language is not regular we use something called a pumping lemma. The pumping lemma cannot be used to show that a language is regular, only that it is not. It is a way to do proof by contradiction - we assume that a language is regular and show that any machine that accepts it would also accept strings that are not in the language.

Consider the language $L = \{a^n b^n\}$ (that is, any number of "a"s followed by the same number of "b"s). Suppose that this language is regular; then there exists a finite automaton that accepts it. This automaton has a finite number of states; call it k. Then if it accepts a string of length k or greater, the same state must be visited more than once (there is a cycle).

We'll take the string $a^k b^k$, which is clearly in the language. Since our machine accepts the language, it accepts $a^k b^k$. However, because we have as many "a"s as the number of states, there must be a loop of size j[5] that we follow in accepting this string. We follow that loop one additional time when reading in "a"s, which leaves us in an accept state for the string $a^{k+j} b^k$, which is clearly not in the language. This contradicts our assumption that we have a finite automaton for the language and shows

---

[5] $|j| > 0$

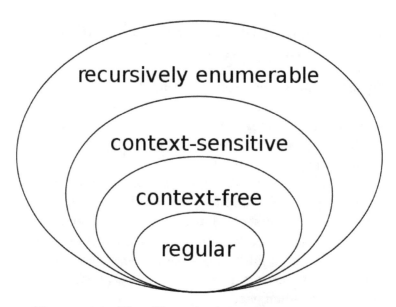

Figure 13.7: The Chomsky hierarchy. The regular languages are a proper subset of the context-free languages, which are a proper subset of the context-sensitive languages, which are a proper subset of the recursively enumerable languages.

that the language is not regular.

13.3 Context-free languages

The context-free languages are a superset of the regular languages - that is, every regular language is also a context-free language. This is part of the Chomsky hierarchy of grammars, in which each grammar properly contains the less powerful grammars in the hierarchy.

Like the regular languages, the context-free languages can be described in terms of the automata which can recognize them, the grammars which can produce them, and the closure properties of the set. The context-free languages are more powerful than the regular languages because they are allowed a memory, specifically an (arbitrarily large) stack. Intuitively, the context-free languages are those in which you must remember at most one thing at a time, so (as we shall prove shortly) $a^n b^n$ is context-free, but $a^n b^n c^n$ is not.

13.3.1 Pushdown automata

A pushdown automata (PDA) is very similar to a finite state machine, with two differences. In addition to looking at the next element of the input to determine which transition to take, it can use the top element on the stack. It can also manipulate the stack as part of the transition.

Like a finite state machine, a pushdown automata consists of a finite set of states (one or more of which may be accept states) with transitions between them. In addition to reading a letter from the input, however, these transitions may pop a variable from the stack and push one or more variables on the stack. In addition to the alphabet of terminals, we have a set of stack symbols (sometimes including a special symbol, generally Z, to denote the bottom of the stack).

A PDA can accept a string in two different ways. The first is by final state, as with the finite automata: the PDA accepts a string if after reading in the string the automaton is in an accept state. A PDA can also accept by empty stack. We can express the same languages using either acceptance method, but it is generally convenient to assume that the PDA must be in an accept state and also have an empty stack; we follow that convention here.

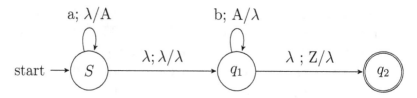

Figure 13.8: A nondeterministic pushdown automaton that accepts the language $L = \{a^n b^n\}$. Here it is assumed that we start with Z on the stack.

Consider the PDA in figure 13.8. In the first state, S, we can read in any number of as (including zero). For each a we read in, we pop nothing and push an A on the stack. When we are done reading in as, we take the λ transition (which reads, pushes, and pops nothing) to state q_1. In state q_1 we read in as many bs as desired, provided that we pop an A from the stack for each b read. Once we have finished reading in the input, we take the final λ transition to the accept state, popping the bottom of stack symbol in the process.

As with finite automata, PDAs can be deterministic or nondeterministic. A PDA is nondeterministic if for a given situation (the current state, the next character in the input, and the variable on top of the stack) there are multiple transitions that could be followed. A deterministic PDA will have at most one transition out of each state that could be followed given the next character of the input and the top character of the stack.

Unlike finite automata, deterministic and nondeterministic PDAs are not interchangable. The nondeterministic PDAs can accept any context-free language, while the deterministic PDAs accept the proper subset of deterministic context-free languages.

13.3.2 Context-free grammar

A context-free grammar, which generates a context-free language, is a grammar where the left-hand side (LHS) is always a single variable, and the right-hand side (RHS) can be any number of variables and terminals. This is a superset of the regular grammars, which still require the LHS to be a single variable but in which the RHS is always exactly one terminal followed by (or preceded by, for a left regular grammar) zero or one variables. Intuitively, the context-free grammars are those in which (because the LHS in a rule of a context-free grammar is always a single variable) a given variable can always be turned into any of its possible replacements, without respect to anything (the context) that might come before or after it.

$$S \to aSb$$
$$S \to \lambda$$

Figure 13.9: A context-free grammar which generates the language $a^n b^n$.

13.3.3 Pumping lemma for context-free languages

As with regular languages, we can show that a language is not context-free by choosing a string that is in the language and then showing that any push-down automata that generates this string must also generate strings that are not in the language. The pumping lemma for context-free languages states that if a language L is context-free, every string s in L that has length of p or more can be written as $s = uvwxy$, such that the following conditions hold:

1. $uv^n wx^n y$ belongs to L for all $n \geq 0$

   This says that if we repeat v and x the same number of times (including zero), we still get something that belongs to the language. We can do this by using the stack to keep track of the number of times we take the first loop and take the same number of iterations through the second loop.

2. $|vwx| \leq p$

   This says the the number of characters in the cycle, including the nonrepeating part (x), is at most p.

3. $|vx| \geq 1$

   This says that the repeating part of the cycle contains at least one character.

In other words, suppose a language L is context-free; then there exists a pushdown automata with p states that accepts it. If a string in the language has length at least p, then the path taken to accept the string must contain a loop of length at least one. If we choose to follow that loop additional times, or not follow it at all, we should finish in the same end state and so we have another string that must also be in the language. If it is not, then this contradicts our initial assumption that we had a pushdown automata which accepts L, and L is not context-free.

The tricky thing about using the pumping lemma for context-free languages is that there are generally multiple ways a string could be broken up such that it follows the rules above, and we must show that any way the string can be broken up still allows us to pump out of the language. Thus, the key to using the pumping lemma effectively is choosing good strings that do not have too many choices at this stage.

For example, consider the language $L = \{a^n b^n c^n\}$. We choose a string $s = a^p b^p c^p$. If uvx consists entirely of "a"s, then pumping up will give us more "a"s than "b"s or "c"s, so the string is not in the language; the same argument holds if it consists entirely of "b"s or "c"s. If it contains two characters, then the string will contain more of those two than the third (or less, if we pump down - that is, don't follow the loop at all). It cannot contain all three characters because it has length at most p and there are p "b"s between the last "a" and the first "c". Thus, every way you can legally break up the string allows you to pump it into something that is not in the language, which proves that the language is not context-free.

13.4   Context-sensitive languages

Context-sensitive languages are the next step up in the Chomsky heirarchy, and properly contain the context-free languages. While regular-languages are accepted by finite automata and context-free languages are accepted by pushdown automata, the context-sensitive languages are accepted by *linear bounded automata* (LBA).

An LBA is a nondeterministic Turing machine[6] in which the length of the usable tape is restricted based on the length of the input[7].

Context-sensitive languages are generated by noncontracting grammars, which are grammars that do not contain any rules where the left-hand side is longer than the right-hand side. That is, when using the grammar, the string being rewritten never decreases in length.

$L = \{a^n b^n c^n, n \geq 1\}$ is a context-sensitive language, because it can be generated with the following grammar:

$$S \rightarrow abc$$
$$S \rightarrow aSBc$$
$$cB \rightarrow Bc$$
$$bB \rightarrow bb$$

Figure 13.10: A grammar that generates the language $a^n b^n c^n$, $n \geq 1$.

13.5 Recursive and recursively enumerable languages

The recursive languages are also accepted by Turing machines, but they remove the restriction on the length of tape used. If there exists a Turing machine that will eventually halt on any given input and correctly accepts or rejects strings in the language, that language is recursive.

The recursively enumerable languages are those languages where a Turing machine can enumerate all valid

---

[6]See chapter 14

[7]Formally, the length of the tape is a linear function in the length of the input.

strings - that is, we remove the requirement that the Turing Machine halt if the string is not in the language. If the complement of a recursively enumerable language is also recursively enumerable, then the language is recursive.

Chapter 14

Turing Machines

14.1 The ultimate theoretical computer

A Turing machine is an abstract machine capable of simulating any algorithm. Other models of computation will be faster, use less memory, be easier to program - but no other machine can solve a problem that a Turing machine cannot (so far as we know - this is the Church-Turing thesis).

> **Caveat**
> Whenever we refer to a computer without other qualifications, we mean a classical (that is, non-quantum) computer.

A Turing machine is a state machine which operates on a memory tape of infinite length, divided into discrete cells. The machine has a head which is positioned over a

163

particular cell; when running an algorithm, the machine reads the value of that cell. It may then write to that cell, move the head to the left or right, and put itself into a new state. Another way to think of this is as a two-stack pushdown automata, where one stack represents the tape to the left of the head and the other stack represents the rest of the tape.

Putting various restrictions on a Turing machine can make it equivalent to other models of computation. For example, if the machine is read-only and can only move the head to the right, this is equivalent to an NFA. On the other hand, it has been shown that various relaxations of the restrictions on Turing machines - making them non-deterministic, adding additional tapes, etc - does not expand the class of problems which the machine can solve (although it does affect the number of operations required to solve those problems).

A universal Turing machine - one that can simulate other Turing machines - is equivalent in power (that is, in the problems it can solve) to a real computer (provided that the real computer has infinite memory).

14.2 Constructing a Turing machine

A Turing machine can be drawn much like our finite automata, as a series of states and the transitions between those states. Each transition includes the character to read (if any), the character to write (if any), and whether the head of the machine should move to the left, right, or stay in the same square of the tape. A string is in the language accepted by a Turing machine if processing a tape containing the string will cause the machine to halt in an accept state. It is rejected if there is no valid transition to follow.

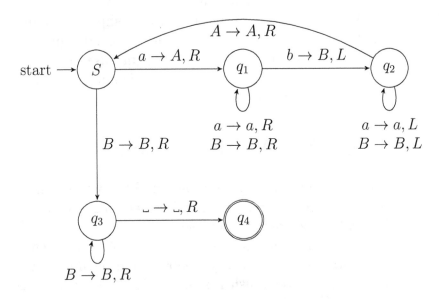

Figure 14.1: A Turing machine for $a^n b^n$. Notice that in the final transition we read an empty square. The machine works by finding an a, matching it with a b, and repeating until it runs out of characters.

14.3 Turing completeness

A system of rules, such as a programming language, is called Turing complete if it can be used to simulate any Turing machine. As a Turing machine can solve any problem which can be solved by a computer, this means

165

that a language which is Turing complete can also solve any problem which can be solved by a computer using any language. Notice that this does not say anything about how long it will take to solve the problem, only that it will eventually arrive at the solution.

An imperative language is Turing complete if it has conditional branching and the ability to handle an arbitrarily large amount of memory, which means that (ignoring hardware limitations) most programming languages are Turing complete.

14.4   The halting problem

If a Turing machine can solve any problem which can be solved by a computer, this implies there are some problems which no computer can solve.

One such problem is the halting problem: given a description of an arbitrary program and an input, will the program ever finish running? This is known as an *undecidable* problem - there is no Turing machine which can answer it for all possible inputs. A machine for a language L will always halt on every string in that language, but may run forever if the string is not in the language and the language is not recursive.

As with NP-completeness, we can demonstrate that a problem is undecidable by showing that deciding it would also allow us to decide another problem that has already been shown to be undecidable.

Afterword

You've reached the end of the first volume! (Well, aside from the appendices.)

At this point you may feel you're not finished - like there's a lot more that you need to know - and you would be correct.

This book is incomplete in two ways. The first is that we have not taken a deep dive into any of the covered topics; had we done so, the book could easily have been three times as long. Instead, I've given you enough understanding to meaningfully participate in conversations about these topics and to search out more information as needed.

The second is that there are many topics remaining to cover: proofs, security, operating systems, networks... the list goes on. You may have noticed cross-references to chapters that do not appear in this book; you'll be able to find them in a future volume. If you've enjoyed this book, be sure to watch for Volume II.

I hope you'll visit my website at `http://www.whatwilliamsaid.com/books/`. There you can find self-assessment quizzes to test your understanding of each chapter, sign up for my mailing list to be notified when the next volume is released (and receive free extra content), and contact me if you have any questions.

If you found this book useful, I would really appreciate it if you could take a minute to leave a review on Amazon. Reviews are a huge help for authors!

Appendices

Appendix A

Necessary Mathematics

How much math do you need for computer science?

The usual gateway class for computer science is algebra; this is because students who struggle with understanding variables in algebra will likely also struggle with variables in programming. As this book is targeted at working programmers, it is assumed that the reader is comfortable with the concept and use of variables.

When analyzing the runtime of an algorithm, we may need algebra and logarithms. The logarithm of a number is the power to which the base (generally 2 for computers) must be raised to produce that number; for example, the base-2 logarithm of 16 is 4, because $2^4=16$.

More advanced topics may also require more advanced mathematics. Computer graphics makes use of multiple imaginary numbers, while machine learning requires calculus and statistics. These topics are outside the scope of this volume.

Unless you're working in a specialized field, algebra, logarithms, and graph theory (covered in detail in Part

II) will generally be all the math you'll need to know.

Appendix B

Classic NP-Complete Problems

This chapter provides a quick overview of some of the classic NP-complete problems. We won't prove NP-completeness, we will simply provide enough detail that the reader may be able to recognize these problems when encountering them. Notice that the problems are described such that we ask whether a solution of size s exists rather than asking for the size of the best solution. This is because the NP-complete problems are defined as decision problems (which have yes/no answers).

B.1 SAT and 3-SAT

The boolean satisfiability problem asks whether, given a formula consisting of boolean variables, values can be assigned to those variables such that the formula is true. For example, the formula "b and not c" evaluates to true when b is true and c is false. On the other hand, no assignments can possibly make the statement "b and not b" evaluate to true.

The formula will generally be written as a series of clauses. For example, if we have a formula that holds true if either of the above statements is true, this would be written $(b \wedge \neg c) \vee (b \wedge \neg b)$. [Read: "$b$ and not c or b and not b".] In this case, each of the clauses contains two literals, but could contain any number. 3-SAT is the same problem with the additional restriction that each clause is limited to, at most, three literals.

B.2 Clique

Given a graph G and a size k, determine whether or not G contains a clique (that is, a complete subgraph) of size k.

B.3 Clique cover

Given a graph G and a size k, determine whether or not G can be partitioned into k cliques, such that every vertex in the graph belongs to at least one of the selected cliques.

B.4 Graph coloring

Given a graph G and a size k, determine whether or not G can be properly colored using only k colors.

B.5 Hamiltonian path

Given a graph G, determine whether there exists a path between the vertices of the graph that visits every vertex exactly once.

B.6 Knapsack

Given a set of items, each of which has a weight and a value, and a knapsack with maximum capacity c, can we find a set of items with value at least v that do not exceed the knapsack's capacity?

B.7 Maximum stable set

Given a graph G, is there a stable set (a set of vertices such that no two are adjacent) of size k?

B.8 Subset sum

Given a set or multiset (a set with repeated values allowed) of integers and a value s, is there a nonempty subset that sums to s? For example, given the set {-7, -5, -3, -1, 4, 8, 156} with $s=0$, {-7, -5, 4, 8} would be one such set.